ADVANCE PRAISE FOR

Never Too Busy to Cure Clutter

"For most of us, outer order contributes to inner calm. We're happier when we're not surrounded by things that don't work, that we don't use, or that are in the wrong place. *Never Too Busy to Cure Clutter* shows that whether we have one minute or an entire weekend, we can make real progress toward curing the clutter that's weighing us down. Turns out, it's not that hard—when we know where to start."

> —Gretchen Rubin, author of *Better Than Before* and
> *The Happiness Project*

"Think you don't have any time to organize your space? Well, Erin Rooney Doland knows you do—and once you follow her advice, you will find it. Whether you are contr   e chaos in thirty-second (really!) bits or devoting la   time to tackle entire rooms, this book walks   s you need to manage your time, and y   as possible. An invaluable tool to help   your house."

> —Kristin van Ogtrop, mana   nd author of
> *Just Let Me Lie Down*

"Finally! A set of clear, doable step   lutter-free life. Erin Rooney Doland provides the perfect balance of guidance and flexibility so readers can transform their homes now—no matter how busy or overwhelmed they are."

> —Asha Dornfest, author of *Parent Hacks* and *Minimalist Parenting*

Never Too Busy to Cure Clutter

never too busy to cure clutter

*simplify your
life one minute
at a time*

ERIN
ROONEY
DOLAND

wm
WILLIAM MORROW
An Imprint of HarperCollins*Publishers*

HarperCollins books may be purchased for educational, business, or sales promotional use. For information please e-mail the Special Markets Department at SPsales@harpercollins.com.

FIRST EDITION

DESIGNED BY WILLIAM RUOTO

Images courtesy of Shutterstock, Inc., Used By Permission

Library of Congress Cataloging-in-Publication Data has been applied for.

ISBN 978-0-06-241972-9

16 17 18 19 20 ov/RRD 10 9 8 7 6 5 4 3 2 1

For Dana and Mike Rooney

THANK YOU

Contents

Using This Book   1

STEP I
CURE CLUTTER ONE ROOM AT A TIME   3

PLACES EVERYONE SEES   8

Entryway   13
WEEKEND PROJECT #1: OPERATION DROP ZONE   18

Living Room   21
Double-Duty Furniture   25
WEEKEND PROJECT #2: CABLE CURE   28

Kitchen   31
*Twelve Things You Already Have in Your Kitchen That
You Can Use to Clean Your Kitchen*   37
WEEKEND PROJECT #3: EXTREME REFRIGERATOR MAKEOVER   41

Bathroom   45
When to Break Up with Your Makeup   49
WEEKEND PROJECT #4: BATHROOM SUPPLIES SHOWDOWN   52

CONTENTS

Dining Room   55
  Quiz: Does Your Dining Room Reveal Your Organizing Style?   59

Spaces Outside Your Home   65

Banish the Mess and Restore Order in Almost Every Room Right Now   69

PLACES ONLY YOU SEE   72

Master Bedroom   75
  WEEKEND PROJECT #5: STEALING IDEAS FROM HOTELS   79

Clothes Closet   83
  Quiz: How to Organize Your Closet   87
  WEEKEND PROJECT #6: FASHION FORWARD   90

Nursery and Young Children's Bedrooms   95
  Teaching Children Organizing, Uncluttering, and Cleaning Skills   98

Preteens' and Teenagers' Bedrooms   101

Home Office   107
  WEEKEND PROJECT #7: CREATE YOUR IDEAL HOME OFFICE   112
  Can an App Do That?   114

Pantry and Food   117
  Meal Planning and the Family Meal   120
  Knife Skills and Mise en Place   123

Hobby Workspace   127
  Wrap It Up!   130
  WEEKEND PROJECT #8: STASH BUSTING   132

PLACES YOU MIGHT NOT WANT TO SEE   134

Laundry Room   137
Ten Tips to Make Laundry Easier   141
WEEKEND PROJECT #9: LAUNDRY BANKRUPTCY   143

Storing Tools and Hardware   147
What to Buy in Bulk   151

Hallways and Stairs   155
WEEKEND PROJECT #10: THE TABLE OF NO RETURN   159

Garage and Automobiles   163
WEEKEND PROJECT #11: A GRATIFYING GARAGE   167

Guest Bedroom   171
WEEKEND PROJECT #12: CREATE A GUEST RETREAT   175

Pet Places   179

STUFF IN ANY OR MANY ROOMS   182

Books and Entertainment   185
**WEEKEND PROJECT #13: DIGITIZE YOUR
BOOKSHELF**   189

Papers, Bills, and Subscriptions   193
Keep It, Scan It, or Shred It?   198

Digital Data and Security   205
WEEKEND PROJECT #14: SECURE YOUR DATA   210

Memorabilia and Collections   213
Is It a Collection or Clutter?   219

Safety and Emergency 223

WEEKEND PROJECT #15: CREATE A MEDICATIONS AND FIRST-AID KIT 227

STEP II
UNCLUTTER YOUR ROUTINES FOR A SIMPLER LIFE 229

Methods for Developing and Maintaining Effective and Efficient Routines 233

Sample Morning Routines 237

Sample Coming-Home Routine 238

Sample Before-Bed Routine 239

STEP III
SURPRISE SITUATIONS THAT CALL FOR UNCLUTTERING 241

Surprise! Guests Are on Their Way 245

TV Is Calling My Name but I Have Stuff to Do 249

The Family Is Hungry and I'm Out of Ideas 253

Weekend Plans Fell Through 257

Glossary of Clutter-Related Terms 261

Acknowledgments 265

Index 267

About the Author 273

Never Too Busy to Cure Clutter

Using This Book

Are you busy? Of course you are! This is an exciting time to be alive, with an unlimited number of things to see and do. Since you're pressed for time, let's dive right into how this book is going to help your home life be less chaotic.

This book has a simple premise: Being organized allows you to make space in your home and life for what really matters to *you*. When you're able to clear the distractions that are cluttering up your time and space, you can eliminate stress and burdens and focus on your priorities.

Think of *Never Too Busy to Cure Clutter* as an organizing daily devotional with more than 450 tips and fifteen weekend projects to help you accomplish your cleaning, organizing, and uncluttering goals. The majority of the information in this book is presented by room and then broken down by time commitment, so you can devote exactly the time you have available to the space you want to address—whether you have only thirty seconds or a full weekend free.

Right now, you are likely feeling overwhelmed by all the stuff and responsibilities in your home and life, and wondering how you can stay afloat. Some of the stuff cluttering up your life might not even be yours! This book is full of advice that has been extensively tried and tested that will help you regain your sanity and find some peace of mind. There's even advice for how to pass along cleaning, uncluttering, and organizing skills to the other members of your family—including kids (so you won't have to spend eighteen years picking up their messes).

But wait! There's more!

In addition to the weekend projects and thirty-second, one-minute, five-minute, and fifteen-minute uncluttering, cleaning, and organizing tasks, this book has fun sections like quizzes, motivation and encouragement from people who are pros at solving clutter problems, and action plans for facing some of life's surprise situations that require uncluttering. I'll even walk you through establishing maintenance routines that will save you time each day with household chores.

I was once in a similar position to yours—quite possibly even more cluttered and more frazzled, if you can believe it. I spent decades living amid so much stuff that there were pathways in my apartment (professional organizers call them *goat trails*) between waist-high piles of boxes. After an inspiring conversation with my husband, I decided to change my ways and learn the skills necessary to have an uncluttered and organized life. I still struggle with wanting to save sentimental objects (my kids draw adorable pictures) and falling behind on chores (laundry is my Achilles' heel), but my days of being a poster child for clutter bugs are ten years in my past. Now I thrive off living my uncluttered life, and you too can find that same calm and order by carrying out the actions in the following pages. You can streamline your life, simplify your daily activities, and make room for what you believe is truly important.

If I do my job well, this book will be a trusty resource that you can rely upon for straightforward, inspiring advice and tips that you can return to time and time again. You also can use this book as a workbook, completing the tasks and working through them repeatedly. My hope is that this isn't a book you read once and forget about—it's a friend you can reference daily.

Yes, you're busy, but you're never too busy to cure clutter.

Step I

CURE CLUTTER ONE ROOM AT A TIME

According to the *Oxford English Dictionary,* the modern English word *organizer* comes from the fourteenth-century Middle French word *organiser.* In this early form, it meant "to give an organic structure to" something. When organizing objects in your home, think back to this early usage of the word and try to create systems that feel as natural as possible. Steer clear of any convoluted system that feels like it includes too many steps or would make it difficult for you to find things or put them away. Know yourself and be honest about your needs and what you will effectively use over the years.

TO DO

get organized

Introduction

It's time to tackle your clutter! Taking the first step of a project can feel intimidating, but there is no need to be nervous about the activities in the following chapters. You can choose simple tasks that can be completed in mere seconds, and be on your way to a less cluttered life without breaking a sweat. Instead of looking at the following actions as an enormous and overwhelming to-do list, try to envision them as encouraging suggestions a good friend might give you while enjoying a cup of coffee—try out the ones you think might work for you and ignore the ones you know won't solve your issues.

There are four parts to the Cure Clutter One Room at a Time step of this book, and each is full of solutions to help you kick chaos to the curb. The first part covers the highest-traffic areas in your home—such as your living room and kitchen. These busy rooms are the foundation for your uncluttered space, so you may want to start in this part. The second part addresses those areas of your home that visitors don't usually see but whose orderliness is still important to making your life easier—like your bedroom and kitchen pantry. The third part is for those areas of the house that you would probably like to forget exist but that need to be kept organized so they don't cause you unnecessary frustration and trouble—I'm talking about your utility areas and storage spaces. Finally, the fourth part covers your important possessions—including your passwords and papers—and how to keep them stored safely and organized.

This entire section provides uncluttering, cleaning, and organizing activities that fit the time you have available. Are you on hold with the pharmacy trying to refill a prescription? Find a thirty-second task you can easily complete while you wait. Have a few hours on a weekend? Take on a larger project that will make the following week easier and even inspire you to do some more simple tasks during the week. Have a teenager who is pleading boredom? A fifteen-minute task might be perfect for him while he brainstorms something else he'd like to do. Watching a live television show and not interested in paying attention to the commercials? A few one-minute tasks can be completed during each break.

Use this book as it meets your needs—being busy doesn't mean you have to live with clutter or disorganization.

WARNING!

We all move at different speeds and have houses of different sizes. How long it will take you to complete a task might vary from the amount of time it takes my clients and me. For reference, I'm a forty-something woman who is accustomed to chasing her two young kids around all day. Also, my home isn't very large. If you notice a task taking significantly shorter or longer than it takes me to do, just make a note in your book so the next time you're hunting for a task you'll remember exactly how long it takes you to complete it.

Places
Everyone
Sees

Geralin Thomas, professional organizer with Metropolitan Organizing and A&E's *Hoarders,* on the benefits of being organized:

Uncluttering, discarding, donating, sorting, categorizing, rearranging, and organizing the stuff in my life makes me feel satisfied and content. When I start noticing too many things in my life that begin with *un-,* it's time to take action and deal with my *un*used, *un*loved, *un*finished, or *un*resolved matters. *Un*tangling my digital, physical, or mental clutter benefits my mind and body. It's simultaneously energizing and relaxing. It's empowering. It improves sleep and self-esteem. It's something I can do all by myself, whenever I want. Being organized has dozens of benefits but one of the best reasons for doing it is because it feels good; there's an afterglow to a good organizing session!

A PLACE FOR EVERYTHING . . .

Throughout the text of this book you're going to encounter references to the Unclutterer motto: "A place for everything and everything in its place." Whenever you see phrases like *proper home* or an object's *place,* it's a safe bet I'm referencing this motto.

What does this motto mean? In short, it means that everything you own—absolutely everything inside your house, car, backpack, etc.—has an assigned place to live, and when it's not in use, that is exactly where you can find the object. For example, pens are stored in a pen cup on your desk in your home office or in a pen cup on the kitchen counter. Pens aren't left on the end table in the living room after they've been used, because that isn't where the pens live. Toilet paper lives on the third shelf of the linen closet or on the holder in the bathroom, and that's it. Toilet paper doesn't live in the middle of the hallway for three days waiting to be put away after a shopping trip, and it doesn't live in the trunk of your car for four months because there was a great deal on toilet paper at the local mega mart that you couldn't pass up and your home lacks sufficient storage for the overage.

How do you decide an object's place? It's best to keep things as close to where they are used as possible. Your shredder should be near the main entrance to your home so you can immediately shred junk mail. If your main entrance is too small to fit a shredder or it isn't feasible for some other reason, find the next-best solution. Put it in the place where it is used the most often that isn't completely frustrating for the other times you need to use it.

Put it on wheels (like the dollies people use for large houseplants) and wheel it around your home, if that's the best solution for you. If you also need a shredder in your office, two shredders might be your answer.

Store the things you access the most often in the easiest-to-access locations. The easier it is to get something out and put it away, the more likely you are to do just that. If you need a pen every time you answer your desk phone, then store a pen right next to your desk phone. And don't go storing heavy things above shoulder height, because you don't want to drop stuff or injure your back.

Realistically, is anyone in the world capable of living with everything in its place constantly? No. We're all human. But it's a terrifically uncluttered ideal, and it's what unclutterers strive to achieve.

Is there a cute acronym I could use? Why, yes, there is. It's PEEP. Adorable.

Entryway

The entryway is the first place you see when you come home and the last place you see when you leave. Your entryway should welcome you with a sense of calm and send you out into the world with a smile on your face.

When working in this area, ask yourself: *What can I do to make leaving and returning home easier? How can I organize this space to get out the door on time with everything I need every time I leave?*

TEN ORGANIZING TOOLS TO HELP YOUR ENTRYWAY RUN MORE SMOOTHLY

1. A hook, bowl, or designated area for your keys
2. A closet, hooks, or stand for your coats and jackets
3. Inboxes for every person who lives in your home so they can find their mail and important papers
4. A trash can
5. A shredder
6. A recycling bin
7. A receipt spike, zip-top bag, or clear plastic envelope to hold your receipts until you can process them
8. A bank for your pocket change
9. Baskets or bins for scarves, gloves, hats, dog toys, and leashes
10. Boxes or bins to hold items you'll need for errands, like library books and charitable donations

30 SECONDS

❑ Sort mail into three piles: Keep, Shred, or Recycle. Repeat this process daily until your backlog is sorted. (See Sample Coming-Home Routine, page 238.)

❑ Sort this week's receipts into three piles: scan for personal records, scan for business records, or shred. Anything needing to be scanned goes to your inbox. Repeat this process until all receipts have been sorted.

❑ Untangle the heap of dog leashes/tote bags/scarves and store them on a hook or in a basket, bin, or cubby.

❑ Look at the inside brims of hats, and at your scarves and gloves. If any need to be cleaned, pack them up for the laundry or dry cleaner.

❑ Clean out the pockets of a coat or jacket—you never know what you might find.

WHAT'S IN YOUR POCKETS?

Whether it's change found underneath the couch cushions, a check found in a pile of papers, or a twenty-dollar bill in the pocket of a winter coat, you're almost certain to find a little money while cleaning and uncluttering. The two biggest finds I've heard about come from Maryland-based professional organizer Jackie Kelley, who helped a client find $1,200 in a single day, and Tennessee-based professional organizer Julie Bestry, who worked with a client who found more than $5,500 during a whole-house project.

1 MINUTE

❏ Match gloves into pairs. Those that have seen better days or are missing a mate can go into your stash of rags. (See page 33.)

❏ If you use a bowl or bin for key storage, sort out anything that isn't a key from the bowl or bin and return it to its proper storage location or to the trash.

❏ Create labels for inboxes, bins, or baskets indicating their function or assignment (*Bob's Inbox, Gloves, Charitable Donations*).

❏ Inspect your briefcase, backpack, or diaper bag to ensure it's in good shape. If it needs to be repaired, schedule a drop-off time with a local tailor.

❏ Move all the empty hangers in your coat closet to one end of the rod for easy access.

5 MINUTES

❏ Sort through the shoes in this area and put away any that should be stored elsewhere. While transporting the shoes, inspect their tips, soles, and heels for damage. Do they need to be shined? Taken to a cobbler?

❏ Open mail from your Keep pile and annotate directly on it future actions that need to be taken: "Pay bill by X date," "Send a thank-you card," "File in Automotive," "Read by X date," etc.

❏ Time yourself to see how long it actually takes you to get out the door each morning once you've decided to leave. Putting on your shoes and coat, gathering up your things, finding your keys, etc., may be taking you longer than you think. Once you know how long it takes you to leave, you can make adjustments to where and how you store your items to better plan your mornings. (See Weekend Project #1 on page 18 for more detailed advice.)

❑ Round up all the keys in your house and label them. Old keys you no longer need can be recycled with other metals.

❑ Clean out your backpack, bag, and/or purse. Throw away trash, shake out crumbs, and only return items to the bag that should be permanently stored there.

15 MINUTES

❑ Return books to the public library, drop off extra wire hangers at the dry cleaner for recycling, and/or take donations to your favorite charity.

❑ Take a full container of spare change to the coin machine at your bank and convert it to paper money or deposit it into a savings account.

❑ Sort through coats and jackets and decide if you should keep or donate each item. Does it fit? Do you wear it? Does it need to be cleaned or repaired? Is it in season, and if so, should it be stored in the entryway—if not, should it be moved to another closet? If you have room, hang up out-of-season coats in bedroom closets so there will be space to hang guests' jackets/coats in the entryway.

❑ Make a list to remind yourself what to restock in a bag when you get home. This idea works well for diaper and activity bags (like beach bags) as well as briefcases. If you use a diaper while on an outing, a list can help you remember to replace it so you're fully stocked and ready to go the next time you leave your home.

❑ Store a broom, dustpan, lightweight cordless vacuum, and/or sponge mop in a closet near your front door. The floor near your main entrance usually needs to be cleaned more often than other floors in your home. By keeping the cleaning supplies nearby, you're ready to go whenever you have fifteen minutes to spare!

Operation Drop Zone

Is your coat on the back of a chair? Are your shoes in the middle of the living room floor? Has a few days of mail morphed into an enormous pile on your dining table? Is it safe to say you would need a few minutes to locate your keys?

If you answered "yes" to any of the above questions, your entryway may need an overhaul. The entrance to your home is the front line for preventing clutter from making its way deeper into your house and for processing all that you're carrying when you get home. In addition to being a drop zone for your stuff, it's also a launch pad for when you're ready to go out into the world.

Whether you're working with a full mudroom or just a console table at your entryway, you'll want to create a drop zone that meets your needs.

WHAT YOU'LL NEED: A charging station for your mobile devices; an umbrella stand; a durable and washable indoor/outdoor rug; hooks or cubbies for backpacks, bags, and/or briefcases; a bench to sit on when taking off or putting on shoes; a tray for muddy and/or wet shoes; a hamper for dirty athletic clothing and/or outerwear; containers for sports equipment; a message board; and a stack of sticky notes and a pen for leaving yourself reminders.

GET IN THE ZONE!

To begin, gather the supplies you'll need from the list above and the one on page 13. Next, clear out the entire space where the drop zone will be. Clean the walls and floors, and get the space ready for your project. Finally, build it and enjoy!

Once your drop zone is up and running and meeting your needs, you'll instantly notice how much of your time and sanity you save by being able to calmly get out the door.

Living Room

Living rooms are the spaces where we kick up our feet after a long day at work, share a good laugh with family and friends, and feel most comfortable in our homes. This may also be the space where you knit a sweater, enjoy a nightcap, check your fantasy football stats, watch a television show, or build a blanket fort with your kids. When in use, these rooms can look like they have been hit by a tornado. But when reset, they're ready for whatever *living* needs to be done in these spaces.

When working in this area, ask yourself: *Is there anything in this space that distracts from people coming together? Is there anything that prevents relaxation? Daily messes are part of living in these rooms, but are there ongoing messes that are difficult to clear before going to bed each evening? What can be done to eradicate the perpetual messes?*

30 SECONDS

❏   Clean the television remote and the front of the television with a soft cloth.

❏   Dust a single shelf, the mantel, the tops of picture and mirror frames— whatever fits in thirty seconds.

❏   Look at the artwork and photographs displayed in the room. Do you still love each item? Does it make you happy? Does it reflect who you are and the life you want to lead? Anything you don't love, take down immediately. When you have more time, sell the artwork or give it away. (An off-the-wall donation idea: Some public libraries allow patrons to check out artwork the same way as books, so consider contacting your local library to see if they would be interested in the artwork you no longer want.)

❏ Lift cushions off your couch and chairs and remove any surprises you find. As a reward, keep any change you unearth.

❏ Gather a wayward item, like a drinking cup or pair of shoes, and return it to its proper home.

1 MINUTE

❏ Remove all out-of-place items from a shelf or tabletop and return them to their proper homes.

❏ Look at your furniture and its layout. Does it promote comfort and good conversation? Does it create the opportunity for a relaxing time for yourself and others? If not, schedule further time (an hour or more) on your calendar to rearrange your furniture.

❏ Grab a yardstick or other long, flat item and fish out anything underneath your furniture that doesn't belong there.

❏ Inspect blankets and/or throws you store in this room. Do any need to be laundered or repaired? If so, put them in a clothes hamper or prepare them for drop-off at a dry cleaner/tailor.

❏ Return video games, DVDs, or any other type of media that has been left out to its appropriate storage case.

5 MINUTES

❏ Alphabetize sheet music and music books on a shelf.

❏ Gather knickknacks, coffee table books, and candles. Inspect them for wear and purge any items you no longer love.

❏ Do a magazine sweep of the room and recycle all old issues. (If you haven't read the magazine in three months, will you ever?) Scan favorite articles or find and save them online and then recycle the issues.

❏ Delete shows you'll never watch from your DVR queue.

❏ Sweep ashes out of the fireplace and into a metal bucket or inspect ceramic logs and stones for cracks and damage.

15 MINUTES

❏ Pull cushions off couches and chairs and vacuum them. Pull out the hideaway bed (if applicable), inspect it for damage, and vacuum the mattress. Flip the cushions on the couch.

❏ Label all electronic cables so it's obvious which cord belongs with which device. If you need to cure a mess of cables, check out Weekend Project #2: Cable Cure (page 28).

❏ Open drawers and wipe or vacuum out dust and grime. Oil, wax, or appropriately repair any drawers that don't open and close easily.

❏ Unclutter and organize all drawers and shelves in coffee tables and end tables. Remove all items that aren't used in the immediate vicinity of the tables and find new homes for those things closer to where they are used. Remember that drawers and shelves don't have to hold anything. If you don't regularly use things here, don't store things here. However, for what you choose to use and store in this space, outfit drawers with drawer organizers to help contain these items.

❑ Are socks, board games, or other items that belong in other rooms constantly being left in this space? Bring in a discreet hamper or storage container to create a temporary home for these items. Then incorporate cleaning out this container once a week into your before-bed routine (see page 239).

CAN'T LIVE WITH IT ANY LONGER?

What area of this room bothers you the most? Why? Sit down and brainstorm what specific steps you can take to alleviate your frustrations. Do the first step now—grab a trash bag and throw out obvious trash like junk mail or simply put away whatever item is at the top of the pile—and then schedule some time to address the remaining necessary actions.

Double-Duty Furniture

In the spirit of surrealist painter René Magritte, it can be useful to envision pieces of furniture and other design elements as something other than what they initially appear to be. When considering furniture that can serve double duties, be creative—you may find a perfect storage solution in an unexpected place.

- **OTTOMANS:** The interior of an ottoman can become blanket storage or even a miniature home office. If the interior space is large, you can subdivide it with boxes and bins. I've even seen ottomans outfitted with rods for hanging file folders.

- **COFFEE TABLES AND END TABLES:** These tables clearly can provide additional storage when equipped with drawers, cabinets, racks, and shelves. If your coffee/end table doesn't provide any storage, you can always create additional storage with decorative trays, boxes, and bins. Make an instant table skirt to conceal items stored underneath by applying a little Velcro on the lip of the table and attaching some fabric.

DIY TIP:
CREATE A CONCEALED CHARGING STATION

If your end table has drawers or doors, you can drill holes in the wood at the back through which you can run wires for remote and mobile device chargers.

- **SHELVING:** Setting up coordinating boxes and bins on shelves is an easy way to disguise loose objects that you need in a room. Most bookshelves also can be outfitted with cabinet doors as another way to keep objects out of view. A quick trip to a home improvement store or Ikea will help you find shelving solutions.

- **BUFFETS:** You usually think of buffets and sideboards as being furniture for a dining room, but nothing is preventing you from putting these pieces in other rooms. Their height is often perfect for setting up against the back of a couch or to use as a media center for a television and/or stereo equipment.

- **DECORATIVE ELEMENTS:** Vases not being used for flowers can hold pens, spare change, or your keys. Fancy boxes can hold books of checks on your desk, stamps, or scissors. Adorable cookie jars in kitchens can hold things other than cookies (I store onions and garlic in mine). Stylish hatboxes and baskets can hold magazines. Antique wood ladders can be used for holding blankets and quilts on the rungs.

- **COUCHES:** A hideaway bed is an obvious suggestion here. Some couches have hidden compartments in their armrests, too, for storing television remotes and other small electronics.

HOW MANY VASES IS TOO MANY?

A good rule of thumb is to never have more vases than you have flat surfaces where you regularly display floral arrangements. Let's say at some point in the past you have put flowers on the coffee table, an end table, a fireplace mantel, a hall table, a bookcase, and a dining room table. In this example, you would only keep six vases. Extras can be sold or donated to charity or floral shops.

Cable Cure

For this project you don't need anywhere close to a full weekend, but you will need a couple of hours to unclutter the mess of cables behind your media center. You'll also want to do some preparation work to ensure you have the right supplies on hand before you begin.

WHAT YOU'LL NEED: Velcro cable ties and/or plastic zip ties (see box on page 29), silver and black fine-tip permanent markers, and 3M Command Cord Clips or equivalent (Command clips are movable, which is why I recommend them). If you don't love your handwriting, skip the markers and purchase cable labels or printable identification tags.

UNCLUTTER YOUR CABLES!

1. **CREATE A WORKSPACE.** Move your desk or media center away from the wall a bit so you can easily reach the back of your equipment. Don't unplug anything. It will be much easier to mark your cables when you can see exactly where they belong.

2. **MARK BOTH ENDS OF EACH CABLE TO IDENTIFY IT.** I prefer to write directly on the cable because you can't lose a tag if there isn't one to lose. Use a silver pen for black cables and a black pen for white cables. If you prefer printed labels, print one up and wrap it around the end of the cable. You might identify an audio cable for your speaker system that attaches to your receiver with LEFT SPKR▶RCVR on the speaker end and RCVR▶LEFT SPKR on the receiver end. The power cable for your receiver might just say RECEIVER PWR on both ends.

3. **TAKE A LOOK AT YOUR EQUIPMENT.** Is it exactly where you want it to be? If it is, leave it alone. If it's not, move it.

4. **WIND UP SOME OF THAT SLACK.** If any of your cables are longer than necessary, wrap up the excess length with either a Velcro cable tie or a zip tie

(don't zip it too tightly at this stage, in case you want to adjust the length an inch or two). You could also install custom-length cables from somewhere like Monoprice.com or your favorite electronics store.

5. **DIRECT ALL YOUR CABLES INTO ONE SPOT.** On to the most fun step of the project! Install the 3M Command Cord Clips to the back of your media center or desk and decide the best spot for your cables based on your preferences—behind a leg of the desk, near the outlet, behind a support beam, etc. Then, bundle the cables together using Velcro cable ties or zip ties. I recommend placing the ties every foot or two.

6. **ASSESS THE SITUATION.** You may choose to use more Cord Clips to feed your cables to the surge protector and then the cable to the outlet. You may also choose to put your surge protector inside a well-ventilated cord-management box (like a Bluelounge CableBox) if it's not hidden behind a piece of furniture.

7. **RETURN YOUR FURNITURE TO ITS PERMANENT LOCATION.** Enjoy not having a nest of cables cluttering up your room.

WHICH CABLE TIE IS RIGHT FOR YOU?

I have it on good authority from a respected home automation specialist that zip ties are the preferred method for bundling cables—zipped snugly, but not too tightly, with the excess tie cut down to the nub—even for high-end insulated cables. Velcro ties are good for people who change out their cables often, though they slip around more than zip ties.

Kitchen

Eating and drinking, cooking and mixing, sharing and celebrating—these are the ways of the kitchen. Having a clutter-free kitchen helps you achieve all these purposes without fuss or frustration. (No one wants to waste time having to search for ketchup in a sea of condiments.) It also allows you to be more aware of the contents of your kitchen so you can plan more healthful meals—and more healthful meals mean you will have more energy to complete all the things you want to do over the course of your day.

When working in this area, ask yourself: *What can I do to make it easier to prepare meals in this space? Are there items on the counter I don't regularly use that could be stored in a cabinet or pantry, or in another room? Is there anything distracting me from preparing, serving, consuming, or cleaning up after a meal?*

30 SECONDS

☐ With a recently disinfected sponge (see page 40), wipe down countertops and the outside of any containers and small appliances.

☐ Sharpen a knife or two. If you don't already own a knife sharpener, get one—sharp knives result in easier food preparation and fewer accidents.

☐ Is anything collecting mold in a bread box, cookie jar, or other storage container? Throw it away.

☐ Grab anything that doesn't belong in the kitchen and return it to its proper storage location.

❏ Throw out any food in your freezer that is no longer safe to eat. How do you know if the food in your freezer is safe to eat? Get in the habit of writing the date you put the item in the freezer directly on the food packaging so you can make better decisions about when to use what you've purchased going forward. Nothing is good after the year point, so start by getting rid of any food items stored longer than twelve months. (Log on to http://stilltasty.com for toss dates on specific items.)

1 MINUTE

❏ Put away clean, dry items from the dish rack or dishwasher.

❏ Look at linens (hand towels, washcloths, napkins, placemats, table-cloths, table runners, etc.) and pull out any with stains or holes to be added to the rag pile.

❏ Wipe down a countertop, cupboard, or drawer front.

❏ Round up measuring spoons and cups and nest them by size.

❏ Unplug your toaster or toaster oven. Pull out the crumb tray from your toaster and empty the bread crumbs into the trash, then wipe down the tray and return it to the toaster. If your toaster doesn't have a tray, turn the whole appliance upside down over the sink or a trash can and shake out the crumbs.

USES FOR THE RAG PILE

Once you send old T-shirts and linens to the rag pile, don't forget to use your rags around the house. Rags are great for cleaning up spills, polishing things like shoes and silver, dusting, removing cobwebs, wiping scuffs off walls, protecting your hand from having to touch something icky, washing your car, and wiping down outdoor furniture.

5 MINUTES

- ❏ Lightly run your finger along the rim of every glass and mug to make sure none are chipped or cracked. Recycle any that are damaged.

- ❏ Load and run the dishwasher or wash a load of dishes in the sink.

- ❏ Inspect all your plates, bowls, and saucers. Throw out any that are damaged or stained. If there are any that are in good shape but that you no longer want, put them in a box to take to a charity that needs them. Schedule time on your calendar to make the donation.

- ❏ If you have multiple sets of plates, spend a few minutes thinking about how often you use them and whether it's worth sacrificing storage space for all of them. Only you know the answer to this question. But if there's a set you never use, selling it or giving it away might be more valuable to you.

❑ Look at where your supplies are stored. Are trash bags in close proximity to the trash can? Are your coffee mugs near your coffee maker? Are your pot holders near the oven? If not, work in five-minute spurts to rearrange items so your kitchen is more convenient to use.

15 MINUTES

❑ Sort through food storage containers. Recycle any that are damaged. Consider repurposing any without lids or only lids for nonfood work (as a paint or varnish cup, desk drawer organizer, puzzle piece tray). Then, organize the remaining items: Store like items with like items, nested inside each other if possible, and order lids by size.

❑ If you have a built-in desk in your kitchen (or if your kitchen table or counter resembles one), give it a solid uncluttering—get rid of outdated calendars and flyers, toss expired coupons and junk mail, and shred sensitive but unnecessary papers. Remove anything that doesn't belong in this space and return it to its proper home. Put important reference papers in plastic sleeves in a three-ring binder. Create folders, notebooks, or cubbies for everyone in the house so they know where to find their important information.

❑ Store your cookbooks and recipes in an area adjacent to the kitchen to avoid potential spills. Purge any that you haven't accessed in years. Digitally scan your absolute favorite recipes so that you have backup copies. Organize what you choose to keep by cuisine.

❑ Pull everything out of a drawer and clean up any crumbs or spills inside the drawer. Before returning items to the drawer, decide if you wish to keep each item. Donate unwanted items to a charity. When returning the items you wish to keep to the drawer, group like items together—forks with forks, spatulas with spatulas, etc.

❏ Clean the removable filter/screen on your oven range's exhaust fan. Soaking it in dish detergent and water for ten to fifteen minutes is usually all you need to do to remove the grease.

LUNCH MAKING MADE EASIER

If you make sack lunches on a regular basis, consider creating a lunch-making kit. In a tray, caddy, or basket, have all the materials (reusable bags, food storage containers, etc.) that you use to make sack lunches. This might mean you have duplicates of some items in your kitchen, but for speed and efficiency, this might be an exception to consider.

IMPLEMENTING A SPONGE SYSTEM

Sponges are moist, warm breeding grounds for bacteria, but they're also incredibly convenient to use in the kitchen. Regular runs through the dishwasher and microwave can help combat the bacteria issue, but how long should you hold on to one? And how many should you have in your kitchen at a time?

Personally, I recommend three: one for dishes, one for counters, and one for cleaning up spills on the floor. Sponges start their lives as dish sponges and are used exclusively for dishes until they begin to show obvious signs of use. Then, I use a pair of scissors and clip one corner off the sponge and it becomes the counter sponge. When it really starts looking like it has seen better days, I clip off a second corner of the sponge and relegate it to cleaning up spills on the floor.

Finally, when it has given all it can give, I trash it or compost it (based on the sponge's material—some are biodegradable). I learned the corner-cutting tip many years ago from a reader, and it's so obviously helpful that even my six-year-old son knows which sponge is which.

Twelve Things You Already Have in Your Kitchen That You Can Use To Clean Your Kitchen

1. **WHITE VINEGAR** It stinks, but it's inexpensive and often does a better job than the nonstinky products on the market. Crack a window while you work and the smell will quickly dissipate. A mixture of ½ cup white vinegar and 1 gallon water will clean your wood, linoleum, and no-wax vinyl floors. The same mixture also makes a streakless window cleaner. Create a paste with 1 tablespoon salt and ½ teaspoon white vinegar to clean your chrome faucets—scrub the faucet with the paste, rinse it off, polish it up, and watch your faucet shine.

2. **BAKING SODA** An opened box of baking soda absorbs bad smells in your refrigerator by neutralizing odors. After it has been in there for a couple of months, you can switch it out for a new box and use the old one as a cleaner. Instead of spending hours scrubbing a pot or pan to remove stuck-on food residue, bring a few inches of water and a couple of tablespoons of baking soda to a rolling boil, turn off the heat, and let the liquid cool in the pan. A light scrubbing with a sponge will easily remove whatever the baking soda didn't dissolve. A mixture of ¼ cup baking soda, ½ cup white vinegar, and a teaspoon or two of water is great for cleaning kitchen sinks—even porcelain ones.

3. **BOILING WATER** If food is stuck on any surface—a plate, a pan, your stovetop, the counter, a glass tabletop—boiling water can be a simple first step to a cleaning project. Carefully pour enough boiling water on the mess to just cover it, wait

a few minutes for the water to cool, and then wipe it up with a sponge. You'll be surprised at how often boiling water will completely take care of the mess.

4. **LEMON JUICE** Like vinegar, lemon juice is an acid that is a helpful cleaner and disinfectant. Mix the juice from half a lemon with a couple tablespoons or more of baking soda, and you can clean the tarnish off your copper pots and pans. Mix the juice from half a lemon into a paste with three or more tablespoons of coarse salt to disinfect and clean wooden cutting boards and butcher blocks. Scrub the surface vigorously, let the solution sit for 10 minutes, scrape the solution off with the abrasive side of a damp sponge, and then clean as usual with the soft side of your sponge. If you have a fresh lemon, cut it in half and use it like a sponge to scrub off grease that has splattered on your stovetop and backsplash. Finish the job by wiping up the juice with a clean sponge.

5. **STEEL-CUT OATS AND CLUB SODA** This combination makes a good abrasive cleaner, like Comet or borax. You have to use it quickly, though, or it loses its oomph. Create a paste with equal parts steel-cut oats (or plain instant oats in a pinch) and club soda. It's an easy way to clean your countertops and tables—don't forget to wipe with a clean sponge after you've scrubbed.

6. **PLAIN YOGURT** If you have solid brass anywhere in your kitchen, a dollop of plain yogurt (be sure it doesn't contain flavors or sweeteners of any kind) is great for removing tarnish. Rub it on with a clean cloth and then wipe it off with a second clean cloth. If you're nervous about using it the first time, try it out on a small, inconspicuous location to see the magical results.

7. **CANOLA OIL** Dab some canola oil onto a cloth and wipe down grease buildup. For reasons a scientist can explain but I can't, canola oil helps loosen the bonds of oil on surfaces. Once the grease is moving, the vinegar-and-water cleaning solution mentioned earlier will finish the job. Canola oil can also be used to polish stainless-steel pans. Rub it in and then wipe off the excess oil.

8. **OLIVE OIL** If you have solid wood cabinets in your kitchen, a mixture of 2 parts olive oil to 1 part lemon juice makes a nice natural cleaner and wood polish for your cabinet doors. Rub it in, let it soak for 10 minutes, and then buff away any excess oil with a clean cloth.

NOTE

These cleaners are almost exclusively one-time-use products and shouldn't be stored in their mixed states, as they can go rancid. When mixing any ingredients, it's best to use glass (such as Pyrex), plastic, or ceramic bowls, and avoid anything metal so you don't accidentally cause chemical reactions with the containers.

CLEANING HELP DOESN'T STOP WITH FOOD

9. **DISHWASHING SOAP** Any cleaning project that involves removing grease can get a boost from a squirt of liquid dishwashing soap (e.g., cleaning faucets, tabletops, and stovetops).

10. **ALUMINUM FOIL** Line a glass cake pan (only glass will do) with slightly crumpled aluminum foil, shake in a few table-spoons of baking soda in a thin layer over the foil, lay your silver (the real stuff) in a single layer in the pan so it touches the foil, and then pour boiling water into the pan to immerse the silver. Let it cool, and in a few minutes, without any scrubbing, your silver will be free of tarnish.

11. **DISHWASHER** Obviously you know this device is amazing at cleaning dishes, but it's also good for cleaning sponges, ce-ramic and glass cabinet knobs and drawer pulls, and glass globes from light fixtures.

12. **MICROWAVE** Bacteria on a sponge will die quickly in a mi-crowave. Wet the sponge, microwave it on high for two min-utes, and let it cool—the sponge will be disinfected. Often, the steam from the sponge being heated in the microwave will even loosen the gunk built up on the appliance's interior walls. Now that your sponge is clean, wipe down the inside of your microwave with it.

Extreme Refrigerator Makeover

It's not just girls who talk to mice and birds in fairy tales who need makeovers from bibbidi-bobbidi godmothers. Your refrigerator is likely due for a little makeover, too.

What you'll need: Two refrigerator thermometers (get rustproof ones, if you can), large garbage bags, a soft sponge, a bowl of water mixed with at least ½ teaspoon dish detergent, a box of baking soda, clean cotton rags, masking tape, a black permanent marker, a pen or pencil, and a notepad.

THE CLEANOUT

During this part of the project, you're going to have to take everything out and either throw it in the trash (if it's expired) or temporarily store it in the other part of your refrigerator. Store the freezer items in the refrigerator and your refrigerator items in your freezer temporarily as you work.

As you remove each item, you'll want to run through the following steps:

1. Check its expiration/use-by date (if it's not printed on the storage container, visit StillTasty.com to find out the item's shelf life).

2. Smell it (even if the expiration/use-by date has not passed, it could still be past its prime).

3. If it is expired, throw it in the trash.

4. If it is still good, write the expiration/use-by date on the lid with a marker or affix a piece of masking tape to the storage container and write that information on the tape. Store any food you plan to keep in the other part of your refrigerator temporarily.

5. Using your pen or pencil and your notepad, keep track of anything you trash that you would like to repurchase immediately. Use the contents of your refrigerator to help you determine your household's needs.

Once it's empty, clean your refrigerator/freezer in its entirety with the soapy sponge. If a shelf has any sticky or stuck-on bits, sprinkle a little baking soda on top of those spots and scrub with your sponge. Afterward, wipe down the interior with a dry, soft cotton rag.

ON TO THE ORGANIZING

Plan out where you'll store items in your refrigerator and freezer based on your needs. Similar items should go together—condiments with condiments, frozen vegetables with frozen vegetables. Storing similar items together makes it easier to find food and helps you when you're composing your grocery list because you easily know what you have and what you don't.

Move shelves around so that you can actually fit what you need to store. If you have younger children in your home, you may want to use the low shelves to store their favorite items so they can grab them without your assistance. My husband's aunt used to store a small carafe of milk and dry cereal already poured into a bowl on the lowest shelf of her refrigerator so her first- and second-grade children could make themselves breakfast.

You may find that you also need:

- Shallow plastic bins for putting all after-school snacks in one place or grouping all yogurt together

- A small caddy for condiments you use multiple times a week so you simply pull out one thing instead of five or six

- A lunch box supply caddy for the convenience of getting these items out all at once (see page 35)

- A leftovers section if, like me, you're quick to forget about them

- Nonadhesive shelf liners, to make cleaning up drips easier and keep round objects (like oranges) from rolling

- Paper coasters under things like bottles of syrup to collect drips that would otherwise make a mess

- A ridged silicone strip laid flat on a shelf that allows you to stack cans and bottles on their sides to save space

Make standard storage work for you. One space provided for you in a refrigerator that can cause a headache is a set of "crisper" drawers. In many homes, they quickly become "rotting" drawers. If they are removable, consider pulling them out and storing them in the pantry. If not, consider using them to store food that isn't quick to rot (like specialty flours). You can affix erasable labels to the drawers' fronts and write their contents on the labels.

Put the thermometers to use. Place one thermometer in the freezer and one in the refrigerator, as close to the center of the middle shelf as possible. Let the thermometer sit for at least eight hours, then check the temperature first thing when you open the door. Ideal refrigerator temperatures are in the low-to-mid-30°F range, and the freezer should be 0°F or lower. If temperatures are warmer than the preferred ranges, adjust the temperature gauge on your refrigerator and freezer.

In 2014, the U.S. Centers for Disease Control and Prevention estimated that "each year roughly 1 in 6 Americans (or 48 million people) get sick, 128,000 are hospitalized, and 3,000 die of foodborne diseases." Cleaning your refrigerator goes a long way toward preventing you and the people who eat food prepared in your home from becoming victims of foodborne illness.

Bathroom

The loo. The commode. The wash closet, washroom, powder room. The bathroom. Whatever you call it, this is a room none of us wishes to live without. They're also rooms likely to be visited by guests. Keeping them clean, uncluttered, useful, and safe is a top priority.

When working in this area, ask yourself: *Is there anything preventing this room from being clean or safe? How can I make this room accommodating for guests, as well as for those of us who use it regularly? If a person with mobility issues were to come to visit, would he or she be able to move safely in the space?*

30 SECONDS

❏ Replace an empty roll of toilet paper.

❏ Inspect hand soap, body soap/gel, shampoo, conditioner, deodorant, and other hygiene items used regularly to determine if they are nearly ready to be refilled or replaced. Add to your shopping list if necessary.

❏ Fold and/or straighten any hanging towels that look disheveled. If one is ready for the hamper, use it to wipe down the counter and sink first.

❏ Put away any stray items—hairbrushes, toothpaste, floss, etc.

❏ Check the power cable on an item that requires electricity to operate—curling/straightening iron, hair dryer, electric toothbrush, electric razor—and make sure there aren't any cuts, crimps, or signs of damage that could make using the item dangerous.

1 MINUTE

❏ Inspect potpourri or other room fresheners/deodorizers to make sure they still have a fragrance. Dust them, if necessary.

❏ Clean the reusable water glass.

❏ Clean the sink and its faucet.

❏ Sort through hygiene items and discard any you don't use.

❏ If you wear makeup, lotion, and/or sunscreen, quickly look at your supply and throw out any items that are expired, dried out, damaged, or too far gone to use. (See "When to Break Up with Your Makeup" on page 49 for more details.)

5 MINUTES

❏ If you have a bench or seating area in your shower, inspect it for damage. Tighten any loose legs. Make repairs or schedule other work that needs to be completed.

❏ Clean the bathtub or shower stall as well as its faucet and showerhead.

❏ Pull all the items out of a drawer, and with a damp cloth, wipe out the inside of the drawer. Cull any clutter and return only items that belong to the drawer.

❏ Using your hands or a comb, remove old hair from a hairbrush. Discard the old hair and then wash the brush with shampoo, rinse, pat with a towel to remove excess water, and allow the brush to air-dry.

❏ Clean a nonmetal comb by soaking it in the sink in a mixture of water and shampoo. Allow the comb to soak until all the grime has lifted off, rinse it, and then dry it with a towel.

15 MINUTES

❏ Gather up all the dirty towels, washcloths, robes, and bath mats and run them through the wash.

❏ Inspect tile grout in the shower/bath and on the floors. Fill and seal any damaged grout areas. Either allot a larger block of time on the calendar to replace broken tiles or schedule an appointment with a professional to do it.

❏ Inspect the caulk and sealants in the shower/bath and around sinks. Clean and/or replace caulk as necessary. A mild dish-soap-and-water mixture should be enough to clean surface mildew and mold. If it's not, try a mixture of lemon juice and vinegar and let it sit on the mildewed area for ten minutes before scrubbing it off. If neither of these methods works, the mildew or mold may have penetrated into the caulk, and it is likely time to replace it.

❏ Assemble a basket of toiletry items guests might wish to use or take home. Include all those small lotions and shampoos you bring home from hotels and spare toothbrushes from the dentist. See "Are You a Secret Hoarder of Hotel Samples of Lotion and Shampoo?" (page 48) for more details.

❏ Inspect all your towels, washcloths, and bath mats. Move any that are damaged or worn to the rag pile. If you have more than one or two, call your local animal shelter to ask if they are interested in a donation of old linens. They often use these for bathing animals when they come into the shelter.

ARE YOU A SECRET HOARDER OF HOTEL SAMPLES OF LOTION AND SHAMPOO?

I'll admit it—I love the tiny shampoos and lotions hotels provide for guests. First, they're tiny, and who doesn't love tiny things? Second, they're great to have on hand in your home to pack for camping trips or to provide to your houseguests. However, too many of these little bottles can clutter up your cabinets. If you think you've gone overboard, you have many options available to you. First, you can put them in a basket in bathrooms visited by anyone who comes into your home and offer them up as swag. A little "take what you want or need" note lets people know you're cool with them running off with some of your stash. Or, you can round up the bottles and donate them to your local housing shelter.

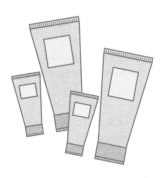

When to Break Up with Your Makeup

With the advent of twenty-four-hour lipstick and foundations that offer all-day coverage, your makeup may last longer than ever before, but how long should you hold on to it? I asked professional makeup artist Emily Amick for her expert advice.

The following time frames for when to toss your makeup are based on the assumptions that you:

1. **KEEP YOUR MAKEUP TO YOURSELF;** that is, don't share it with anyone else.

2. **WASH YOUR HANDS** before touching any of your makeup.

3. **SPRAY YOUR BRUSHES AND SPONGES** with alcohol after every use.

4. **CLEAN YOUR BRUSHES AND SPONGES** with a detergent (like Dawn dish detergent or a baby shampoo) after every other use.

Doing these four things will decrease the amount of bacteria that will get into your makeup, which can cause breakouts and other skin, eye, and mouth infections. These precautions will also improve the quality of your makeup's application.

Bacterial growth aside, the chemicals in makeup degrade over time, and things like air, moisture, and heat can speed up this process. Replacing makeup on a regular schedule is good for many reasons—it's not just the manufacturer trying to move more product. Beyond these guidelines, if at any time you notice a product irritating your skin, eyes, or mouth, immediately stop using it. The same is true for any product that takes on a bad odor or a noticeable change in texture and/or quality.

- **MASCARA AND LIQUID EYELINER:** Because eye infections can have serious consequences, like blindness, it's best to replace liquid eyeliner and mascara every three months.

- **LIQUID FOUNDATION, PRIMER, CREAMY BLUSH, CREAMY EYE SHADOW, AND TUBE CONCEALER:** As long as the consistency is good, you can get by replacing these items once a year. (I like to do it around my birthday so I don't forget.)

- **PRESSED POWDERS, BLUSH, AND EYE SHADOWS:** Replace every eighteen months to two years.

- **LOOSE POWDERS, BLUSH, AND EYE SHADOWS:** These are more likely to get infected with bacteria and degrade more quickly, since all of the product is exposed to the air. Therefore, it's good to replace loose powders every six months to a year (do it at six months if you're especially bad about cleaning your makeup brushes).

- **PENCIL-STYLE EYELINER AND LIP LINER:** As long as you sharpen the pencil to reveal fresh product, you can replace this every other year.

- **LIPSTICK:** Replace once a year. And it doesn't hurt to wipe off the top layer of the stick every couple of weeks with a clean tissue.

- **LIP GLOSS AND WAND-STYLE CONCEALER:** Any time you touch a wand to your face and then stick it back into the product, you're introducing bacteria and saliva into the makeup. Replace these products every six months.

- **MOISTURIZERS:** Similar to liquid foundation, you can usually replace these once a year. However, if the moisturizer is in a large container that you have to dip into with your fingers, consider pouring a portion into a clean, small, airless pump bottle to reduce the amount of bacteria that can get into the larger tub. The pump will also make daily use more sanitary.

- **SUNSCREEN:** Chemicals in sunscreen that protect you from the sun's harmful rays become less effective over time, so replace as the manufacturer recommends on the product's packaging.

Bathroom Supplies Showdown

Similar to a kitchen pantry, bathrooms are places where supplies (like lotions, creams and conditioners, and makeup) linger well past their expiration dates and small containers can be easily lost at the back of cabinets. Additionally, housing beauty, hygiene, and linen supplies all in a small room can make organizing frustrating.

Growing up, my family of four lived in a house with one full bathroom. The room was so small you could stand in the bathtub and touch all of the walls of the room. Storage for the space consisted of one very narrow linen closet and a three-shelf cabinet above the toilet. There was a pedestal sink, so the only thing beneath the washbasin was a trash can. It was . . . cozy . . . and serves as a reminder that a lot can be done with very little space.

Even if you have multiple bathrooms in your home, with ample storage, you still can bring more efficiency to your bathroom. It's time to have a showdown with your stuff.

Getting started: As with so many organizing and uncluttering projects, you'll want to start by clearing the space and then cleaning it. Be careful when you use caustic chemicals to clean the bathroom. To avoid mixing potentially hazardous combinations, I prefer to use basic dish soap mixed with water and a soft cloth to wipe down shelves and containers, and vinegar mixed with water on mirrors and windows. (See page 37 for exact ratios.)

Once everything is out of the bathroom and you've cleaned it and inspected it for damage, you're ready to sort through everything you've removed.

Check expiration dates. Anything that has expired should be thrown in the trash.

Avoid creating bacteria hot spots. Consider throwing away anything that is old that you dip your fingers in to use, like lotions and creams that come in tubs. Bacteria gets into tublike containers relatively easily, and in a warm, damp environment like a bathroom, that bacteria can grow very quickly. Finally, if something doesn't look or smell right to you, toss it. It's much less expensive to replace a twenty-dollar container of your favorite lotion than it is to pay for antibiotics to deal with a skin infection.

Store like items with like items. When returning items to the room and their permanent storage spaces, try your best to store things near where they are used. If you don't like having things on top of your counters, get storage units with handles that can easily be moved as a single kit from a cabinet to the countertop while you get ready, and then back to the cabinet.

You may also find it helpful to think outside the box when it comes to storage solutions for this room. Here are some ideas to get you started:

- **KITCHEN ITEMS**, like a tiered in-cabinet spice organizer, could work at the back of a cabinet for storing hygiene products. Food storage containers with lids can hold bobby pins and hair bands. A drawer organizer can sort brushes, combs, and batteries for your electric toothbrush.

- Empty a large, round **OATMEAL CONTAINER** and cover it with decorative adhesive paper. Wrap headbands around it and put brushes or hair spray inside (take a headband with you to the store to make sure you get the right size container).

- A **PLASTIC PASTA STRAINER** can hold children's bath toys as they dry and then be moved to a cabinet under the sink for storage. (Run the toys through the dishwasher every few months to keep mildew from forming.)

- A **LARGE BASKET** can be decorative in addition to holding spare rolls of toilet paper or rolled-up clean towels waiting to be used.

- **REMOVABLE ADHESIVE HOOKS** can attach to any wall to hold robes or towels. These are especially good for when you have overnight guests and towel rack space is limited.

- **OLD CHECK BOXES** can organize lipsticks, nail polish, or other small items in drawers. Cover the boxes in washi tape to make them cheerful.

- **OVER-THE-DOOR RACKS** can provide additional towel storage. There are also heat-resistant holsters that secure over cabinet doors for hair dryers and curling and straightening irons.

Dining Room

Dining rooms are interesting places in that some people use them three times a day for eating and others *might* use them three times a year for a meal, the rest of the time using the space as a makeshift home office. Irrespective of how often you use the room, keeping it uncluttered, clean, and organized ensures that it's ready to be used whenever you have a need for it. Remember: You're more likely to eat in this space if it's not cramped, cluttered, or arranged in a way that makes it difficult to get to the table.

When working in this area, ask yourself: *Where is the obvious clutter in this space and how long does it usually live there? If the table isn't usually clear of clutter, what can I change about my routines or processes so that it can be regularly used for eating? Do I need a larger desk for my home office space or a better drop zone in my home's entryway?*

30 SECONDS

❑   If you have mail, homework, or other clutter not related to eating on your table, sort through however much you can in thirty seconds and find a more appropriate location for it.

❑   Wipe down the table with a cleaner appropriate for your type of table—a mixture of dish soap and water works on most surfaces.

❑   Clean the seat of a chair with a soft damp cloth and then wipe it with a dry cloth.

❏ Shake crumbs off a few placemats over the kitchen sink.

❏ Shake out the tablecloth or table runner, if you use one.

1 MINUTE

❏ If your table has a centerpiece, wipe it down with a dry cloth or take it outside and shake off the dust.

❏ Set the table with a tablecloth or nice placemats, cloth napkins, and other items used during a meal, as a continual reminder that the table isn't a depository for clutter.

❏ Inspect the legs of your table and chairs to make sure they're in good condition. If they're loose or repairs are needed, schedule time on your calendar to take care of this longer chore.

❏ Refold any cloth napkins that are disheveled in a drawer of a side-board/buffet/china cabinet.

❏ Relocate napkins, placemats, and napkin rings so that they're grouped together in one location, like on a shelf or in a drawer of a buffet near your table.

5 MINUTES

❏ Wipe down the underside of your table and chairs—you would be surprised how much food can get stuck to the underside of these items, especially if you have children eating here regularly.

❏ Evaluate the lighting in this room. Is there enough light? Do you have the ability to dim the lights for a relaxing and/or romantic meal? Do you need other types of lighting? Add a task to your to-do list to acquire dimmable secondary lighting sources for the room if you don't have them already and if lighting is an issue in this space.

❏ If you have uncarpeted floors, attach, inspect, and/or replace felt pads on the bottom of dining room chairs and table legs.

❏ Clean out the clutter from a single drawer or shelf of your sideboard/buffet/china cabinet/wherever you store your dining table supplies.

❏ Put on a pair of polishing gloves (like Hagerty Silversmiths' Gloves) and buff up any pieces of metal, such as brass drawer pulls or silver napkin rings, that may have tarnished.

15 MINUTES

❏ Find new homes for any spare furniture or other items that may be taking up floor space and aren't related to the purpose of this room, whether this means selling the furniture or simply finding a more appropriate place for it in your house.

❏ Create kits of homework/office supplies that you can easily pack away before a meal or take out after one if you often use the dining table as a work surface. Have an official storage place for these kits (not in a pile on the floor!) when they're not in use.

❏ If you have china and crystal you're not using, why aren't you using it? Spend some time thinking about any of these items that you don't use and whether you might be ready to get rid of them. See the "Letting Go of China and Crystal" box for tips on making these decisions.

LETTING GO OF CHINA AND CRYSTAL

If you're not regularly using your china and/or crystal, it might be time to let these items go. For a lot of people, this is a big decision, especially when the china and/or crystal is a family heirloom or was a wedding present. Give yourself time to really consider it and talk it over with anyone who might have a strong opinion about your decision. If you wish to get rid of it, another family member might be interested in it. But if you're not using it and you don't have plans to use it, the china and crystal is clutter in your home.

❏ Place an inbox on the table if you have trouble breaking the habit of dumping mail and other papers onto the table when you come home each day. An inbox is much easier to move than a loose pile of papers. If you go this route, schedule fifteen minutes, at least twice a week, to process the contents of the inbox. (See page 18 for suggestions on keeping loose papers at bay by creating a useful entryway.)

❏ Scrub the floor or steam clean the carpet beneath your dining table and chairs.

QUIZ

Does Your Dining Room Reveal Your Organizing Style?

The choices you make in using and designing your dining room can speak to your overall organizing style. Answer the questions below to determine what type of organizer you are, and read on to garner specific tips that can help you avoid clutter pitfalls specific to your style.

1. **Does all your dining room furniture match (from the same furniture maker, same finishes, same style)?**
   A. Yes
   B. For the most part
   C. Not even close

2. **Does the artwork in the room have a theme (matching frames, all family portraits, all landscape paintings)?**
   A. Yes
   B. No
   C. What artwork? I've got bare walls.

3. **What is the lighting in the room like?**
   A. Lots of lighting sources and natural light
   B. A dimmable chandelier
   C. A chandelier with two settings: on and off

4. **When was the last time you changed the furniture, wall color, or flooring in this room?**
   A. In the last two years
   B. In the last ten years
   C. More than twenty years ago—why change what works?

5. **Do you have carpeting or rugs under the table?**
   A. Yes
   B. No

6. **Do you sweep the floor under the table and chairs after each meal (having your dog lick it clean doesn't count), or do you clean it only when you clean the floors in neighboring rooms?**
   A. After each meal
   B. When cleaning other floors
   C. I don't eat in here, so there's no need to clean in here

7. **How often do you eat at your dining room table?**
   A. Every meal we eat inside the house
   B. Occasionally, like for Sunday dinner and a couple of times during the week
   C. Only when we entertain guests
   D. Never, not even when we entertain

8. **Do you like your dining room?**
   A. Yes, LOVE it!
   B. Yes, it's nice.
   C. I don't have an opinion either way.
   D. Not really, but it could be worse.
   E. No, I hate it!

9. **Do you have items on display in a china cabinet or similar case?**
   A. Yes, with lights, and I've curated the content.
   B. Yes, but just because the cabinet goes with the table.
   C. No, but I wish I did.
   D. No, not my style.

10. **Does your table have leaves?**
    A. Yes
    B. No

SCORING

1. a. 10, b. 5, c. 0
2. a. 10, b. 5, c. 0
3. a. 10, b. 5, c. 0
4. a. 10, b. 5, c. 0
5. a. 10, b. 5
6. a. 10, b. 3, c. 0
7. a. 10, b. 7, c. 3, d. 0
8. a. 10, b. 7, c. 0, d. 3, e. 5
9. a. 10, b. 3, c. 7, d. 0
10. a. 10, b. 0

RESULTS

70-100 POINTS *You pay great attention to details and you like things a particular way.* When organizing, you will likely be able to handle more steps in your maintenance routines than the average person. When organizing closets and places visitors to your home don't see, you'll still go the extra mile for containers to match and the items to look exactly how you desire.

WATCH OUT FOR: Falling victim to wanting things to be perfect.

FOCUS ON: Getting things done.

· Remember that organizing and uncluttering are means to an end, not the end goal. Try to avoid uncluttering and organizing for the sake of uncluttering and organizing. Focus on what is important to you and how having an organized and uncluttered space can help you reach those goals.

· You *can* go the extra mile, but only put in the extra effort after you're finished and are certain you have extra time.

· When/if you feel overwhelmed, reduce projects to their smallest steps. Tackle one drawer, not the entire dresser.

40-69 POINTS *You like things to be organized, but you don't beat yourself up when a little disarray sets in.* You know you'll eventually get things back in order when your schedule permits. The easier things are, though, the more obvious organizing systems are to you, and the more likely you are to complete them. Places visitors see are a higher priority for you than places only people in your home encounter.

> **WATCH OUT FOR:** Clutter blindness—looking at an item of clutter repeatedly may make you oblivious to it.
>
> **FOCUS ON:** Creating routines that help you address your entire home.

- When working on longer uncluttering and organizing projects, consider having an accountability partner to help motivate you. This is especially important in those areas of your home guests don't typically see—like clothing closets and filing cabinets.

- Establish routines that make complete sense to you—load the dishwasher immediately after a meal, wash your face for the night when you change clothes after work (instead of right before bed), put a trash can in your garage so you can clean out the car easily each time you get out of it.

- If asked to take on a new responsibility, try your hardest not to immediately agree to it. Give yourself time to think about how the new responsibility will impact your life. "Let me get back to you tomorrow after I check my calendar" or "Let me think on it awhile—I should have a better understanding of my workload after I talk to my manager this afternoon" are things you might say to give yourself time to evaluate an offer.

< 40 POINTS *As long as something works and doesn't distract you, you're comfortable.* You want your organizing systems to be as simple as possible to create and maintain. You likely don't eat in the dining room because eating in there means you have to spend time cleaning in there, and that isn't something you can fit into your schedule. You tend toward minimalism because having fewer things is more preferable to you than having to organize, clean, and maintain a lot of things.

> **WATCH OUT FOR:** Accumulating too much stuff.
>
> **FOCUS ON:** Uncluttering and reducing the number of things you own.

- Remember that uncluttering isn't a game someone can win. There aren't trophies for the person who has the least stuff, for obvious reasons. When purging clutter from your life, be thoughtful of the process and really consider what you use and what you don't.

- Conversely, beware of keeping clutter "just in case." Owning that item might give you a sense of security, but if you don't have a use for it or it doesn't enrich your life in any way, it's okay to get rid of it. The caveat to this would be any item that helps you manage your responsibilities (such as money saved in a retirement account) or is vitally helpful in an emergency (such as bandages). I'm talking about genuine clutter—like the asparagus peeler you keep around even though you hate asparagus.

- Apathy can be harnessed for good. When in a buying situation, put a pause on any purchase that doesn't make your heart sing. Okay, so this may not apply to trips to the grocery store when you're there to pick up a gallon of milk, but it can certainly work when clothing and furniture shopping.

Spaces Outside Your Home

If you live in a house with a yard, this part of your home is the first glimpse of your property that guests see. If you live in a townhouse, condo, or apartment, there is less for your guests to see, but the places before your front door still make an impression. These areas set the stage for what guests should expect indoors. If your yard, garden, and doorway are inviting, guests will instantly feel comfortable and welcome. It's also nice to come home from work to find outside spaces that calm you instead of creating stress or anxiety.

When working in this area, ask yourself: *Is there anything in the yard that doesn't belong there? Have children left toys out or has a recent storm caused tree limbs to drop? Are there steps I can take now that will make lawn care easier in the future? Are any plants, trees, sidewalks, or other areas a complete eyesore?*

30 SECONDS

❑ Shake out the doormat.

❑ Wipe dirt from the top of your door.

❑ Clean the front door's peephole and wipe down the doorknob with a disinfecting wipe.

❑ Pick up a fallen branch or stick from the yard or sidewalk, and put it in the compost, lawn clippings bin, or fireplace kindling pile.

❑ Wipe spiderwebs and dust from your mailbox with a dry cloth.

1 MINUTE

❏ Brush away spiderwebs and light dirt from the ceiling corners of a porch or balcony.

❏ Wet a soft cotton rag and wipe down your house numbers or unit numbers and the doorbell.

❏ Add water to a birdbath or food to an empty bird feeder.

❏ Put away a child's forgotten toy in the garage.

❏ Inspect the driveway for oil spots. If you find one, see page 67 for how to clean it up.

5 MINUTES

❏ If you have a fence, walk along the fence line and inspect it for damage and/or aging. With a digital camera, take pictures of any places that need to be repaired. Schedule time on your calendar to fix those areas or to hire someone to fix them for you.

❏ Hose off and/or wipe down patio furniture.

❏ Inspect patio furniture for damage or aging. Mark time on your calendar to make necessary repairs or to dispose of irreparable items at the local dump.

❏ Call an arborist and set up an appointment to have your trees inspected.

❏ Pull weeds from around trees, walkways, and porches. Set a timer for five minutes and see how much you can get done in that period. (Remember that next time you think you don't have time for weeding!)

15 MINUTES

❏ Sweep the front walk, stairs, and driveway.

❏ Sweep/mop the porch, balcony, or deck.

❏ Trim branches that are interfering with walking paths.

❏ Clean up oil stains from your driveway. I'm a kitty litter loyalist: Pour kitty litter over the stain, stomp it in, wait a day, then sweep up the litter. I've been told that a good scrub with Pepsi or a mixture of equal parts Dawn dish soap and Murphy Oil Soap will also do the job.

❏ Replace any outdoor lights that have burned out or whose functionality could be improved with motion sensors. Consider new types of lighting that could improve safety, like path and stair lighting. Many brands of these types of small lights are solar powered and don't require wiring.

Banish the Mess and Restore Order in Almost Every Room Right Now

The following are basic actions you can complete in almost every room of your home. Some of these tasks seem incredibly obvious, but it's often the simplest and most conspicuous tasks that form the foundation of your cleaning routine. A few of the following tasks are equally important but only need doing at certain times of the year. Pick and choose your way to a clean, uncluttered, and organized home.

When working in any room of your home, ask yourself: *Where is clutter accumulating? Is there a reason things are piling up in one (or more) area(s)? What would prevent clutter from being left in this space? What small act would greatly improve this room?*

30 SECONDS

❏ Dust one of the following: a single shelf, a picture frame or two, the top of a doorjamb, a lamp, or a light fixture.

❏ Wipe down a tabletop or other flat surface.

❏ Gather wayward pens and pencils and return them to their storage spot.

❏ Clean a doorknob with a disinfecting wipe.

❏ Replace a burned-out lightbulb (preferably with an LED bulb, so you won't have to replace it again for years and will save on energy costs).

1 MINUTE

❏ Find two items that aren't where they belong and return them to where they do.

❏ Clean a mirror, window, the glass front on a cabinet, or picture frame.

❏ Dust a ceiling light/fan fixture, crown molding, baseboards, or a corner of a room with a telescoping duster.

❏ Check your toilet paper and facial tissue inventory throughout the house and replace as necessary.

❏ Change your perspective: Lie on the ground or stand on a step stool to see if you can spot hidden clutter.

5 MINUTES

❏ Empty the trash cans and/or recycling bins in a room.

❏ Round up dirty clothes to start a load of laundry.

❏ Check the batteries in a device. Replace them if necessary.

❏ Move a piece of furniture and sweep or vacuum under it, or vacuum all the air vents in a room.

❏ Fill a basket with wayward items and return those items to their permanent storage locations.

15 MINUTES

❏ Vacuum or sweep the floor of a room.

❏ Fill a bucket with ½ cup white vinegar and 1 gallon water, and mop the uncarpeted floor in a room.

❏ Remove all the fabric curtains in a room from their rods and put them in a bag to bring to your dry cleaner.

❏ Move furniture off a throw rug or hall runner and take the rug outside. Shake it out and then drape it over something (like a railing) and hit it with a broom handle. Return the rug and replace the furniture.

❏ Inspect furniture for damage and wear. Schedule any appointments necessary to have damaged and/or worn items repaired or set aside a block of time to shop for a replacement.

Places Only You See

Gretchen Rubin, author of *The Happiness Project* and *Better Than Before*, on the benefits of the one-minute rule:

I make it a habit to follow the "one-minute rule." If there's something that can be done in less than a minute, I do it without delay. In less than a minute, I can open a letter, scan it, and toss it; I can hang up my coat; I can print a document and file it in the proper place; I can put the newspapers in the recycling.

This rule is effective because no effort takes much time or energy, but by following it, I keep that scum of clutter from collecting on the surface of my life. It's so easy to get overwhelmed by tiny tasks—things that are individually trivial, but in the mass make me feel weighed down and listless.

Of all the things I've suggested related to happiness and habits, this is one of the ideas that seems to resonate most with people.

Master Bedroom

Bedrooms are sanctuaries. They are retreats from the hectic world. When chaos exists in all other areas of your life, your bedroom should be the one place where you can find solace and calm. A well-organized and relaxing space will initiate better sleep, provide refuge, and help you prepare to face the world.

When working in this area, ask yourself: *Is there anything in this space that doesn't promote sleep or relaxation? Are the decorations or designs too busy? Could I remove anything to make the space calmer? What is the first thing I see in the morning, and does that thing instantly bring me joy or serenity?*

30 SECONDS

❏ Make the bed.

❏ Close any drawers or doors that are errantly open, and properly put away any items that may have been hindering the drawer or door from closing.

❏ Pick up any dirty clothes from the floor or piece of furniture and put them in the hamper or a bag to go to the dry cleaner.

❏ Open your sock, underwear, or shirt drawer. Pull out any items with holes, stains, or elastic that is in failure mode and put them in your rag pile or the trash.

❏ Carry any dirty glasses or other dishware from your nightstand to your kitchen so they can be cleaned.

1 MINUTE

❏ Evaluate artwork and decorations to make sure they promote sleep and relaxation. If you spot something that doesn't, schedule time in your calendar to address the issue.

❏ Count the number of decorative pillows on the bed. If you have more than three, consider getting rid of some of the pillows to simplify bed making.

❏ When was the last time you replaced your sleeping pillows? If it has been more than a year, make a note on your shopping list to get new pillows. You should also wash your pillows every few months.

❏ Reset any clock that is off its time and test lightbulbs to make sure they all work. If any are burned out, take another minute and replace them.

❏ Wipe down doorknobs, drawer pulls, and light plates.

5 MINUTES

❏ Unclutter a single drawer in your nightstand and organize it so you can find things easily in the dark. When returning items to the drawer, lie down in your bed and put the most important items in the location that is easiest to reach from your prone position.

❏ Sort through your sheets, blankets, and other bed coverings and inspect them for wear. Anything containing a hole or damaged elastic may be ready to be donated to an animal shelter. Sheets that have lost their set mates, fancy pillowcases, duvet covers, lightweight blankets, heating blankets, and other bedding should be purged or mended if they are showing signs of significant wear.

❏ Designate an area to function as a valet to catch everything you regularly carry on you, such as your watch, a ring, and a pen. If you already have a valet, clear it of any clutter.

❏ Round up all the knickknacks in this space and evaluate them to ensure they don't distract from sleep and that they make you happy. Sometimes having an overwhelming number of objects in the room can interfere with sleep. Keep only those decorative items that support the purposes of this room.

❏ Give attention to your bedroom's shades. The darker the room, the better you sleep, and the better you sleep, the more productive you are the next day. Dust the curtains and blinds you currently have and consider adding thicker fabric to the back of your curtains or dark Con-Tact paper to roller blinds to limit light into this room.

15 MINUTES

❏ Remove the bedsheets and vacuum your mattress. Rotate and/or flip the mattress if it is recommended for the type of mattress you have.

❏ Wash and dry your duvet (and duvet cover) or bedspread—if these items won't fit in your washing machine, take them to a local laundromat with high-capacity washers or to your dry cleaner.

❏ Pull out any storage containers that reside beneath your bed. Evaluate the contents of these containers and decide if anything can be purged. Are you keeping anything you don't use or need? Is under-bed storage the best storage option for these items? When organizing these items and returning them beneath your bed, remember to have the things you need to access most often in the most convenient locations.

❏ Control cables for any electronic equipment in this space—like television, stereo, or cell phone charging cords. See Weekend Project #2: Cable Cure (page 28) for suggestions.

❏ Establish rules for your bedroom moving forward. What types of things will you and won't you allow in this space? This applies to items like food, drinks, knickknacks, electronic equipment, and anything that may influence your sleep.

HOW MANY SHEET SETS DO YOU NEED?

A basic rule of thumb for a four-season climate is to have four sets of sheets for each bed—two for warmer months and two for colder months. This way you can have a seasonally appropriate set clean and ready to go in the linen closet and another set on the bed. If you live in a steady climate, you might be able to get away with two sets. If you live in a small space with little to no storage, and you're great at doing laundry, you might even be able to get by with just one set of sheets for your bed.

As far as guest beds are concerned, you can likely get by with only one set for each season—but if the mattress on that bed is the same size as another bed in your home, you may not need a separate set. Our guest bed (a.k.a. the pull-out couch in our living room) has a queen-size mattress, same as the bed in the master bedroom, so we don't store extra sheets just for the guest bed. Donate sheets you don't need to an animal shelter.

Stealing Ideas from Hotels

There is a sense of calm I get walking into a nice hotel room for the first time. In these rooms, there's no clutter and everything is clean and dust-free. The bed is made, the dresser drawers are all closed, and the room invites me in to take a nap or go to sleep. Each hotel room provides important lessons that you can implement in your home about uncluttering, cleaning, and organizing bedrooms.

IDEAS FROM HOTELS YOU MAY WANT TO IMPLEMENT

- **GOOD LIGHTING, FEW KNICKKNACKS.** Hotel rooms rarely have overhead lighting, but always have zone lighting. Tall lamps are near tables and chairs to provide light for meals and conversations, each dresser and nightstand usually has a table lamp, and each bed has a sconce on each side to provide reading light. Beyond lamps, rooms don't have much else on their table surfaces except for the television, television remote, alarm clock, telephone, and a few pamphlets explaining local and hotel services.

  Can you re-create this in your bedroom (only without the pamphlets)?

- **CALM ARTWORK AND WALL COLORS.** Only in one funky New York hotel have I ever seen artwork hanging in a hotel room that wasn't a landscape or other tranquil composition. The reason the artwork is placid is because the hotel doesn't want you to have enough interest in it to be tempted to steal it, and they don't want it to traumatize you while you sleep. The same standard applies to the neutral colors of the wall paint.

  Can you choose artwork and wall paint for your room that will make you happy when you see it first thing in the morning and will also make you feel comfortable at night to help you fall asleep?

- **SUPPLIES WHERE YOU NEED THEM.** If you need to iron your clothes while staying in a nice hotel, there's an iron in the closet. If you forgot to pack your shampoo, there are bottles in the bathroom for you to use. If you need to charge your phone, there is often an outlet in the base of the lamp on the nightstand. If you need an extra pillow or blanket, they're in the closet near the bed.

When organizing your bedroom, can you store your supplies where you use them?

- **SUN-BLOCKING CURTAINS.** Almost every hotel window has both a sheer curtain that lets light into the room but provides some privacy and a heavier, lined curtain that blocks out all outdoor light into the room. Ample research proves it's easier to sleep soundly when the sun isn't flooding a room with light.

  Can you install sun-blocking curtains on your bedroom windows to make it easier to sleep soundly?

- **NIGHTSTAND WITH STORAGE.** In most every hotel room across the United States there is a nightstand with a drawer next to the bed. In your home, nightstands with drawers are extremely helpful for holding reading glasses, tissues, books, television/stereo remotes, or whatever it is you wish to have next to you when you're in bed. If you share a bed, a nightstand on each side of the bed increases the amount of storage in the room and its functionality. (Drawer dividers are great for keeping your stuff organized inside the drawer.)

  Can you place nightstands next to your bed that have drawers and/or shelves for storage?

Clothes Closet

If clothes make the man (or woman), what does your clothes closet say about you? You don't have to be a fashionista to take care of your clothing and have a well-organized and uncluttered closet. Keeping this space chaos-free will make it easier for you to get ready each morning, reduce your stress and the amount of time it takes to decide what to wear, protect your clothes from unnecessary damage, and ultimately help your apparel, shoes, and accessories last longer. And those are benefits all busy people can support.

When working in this area, ask yourself: *Do I wear every item stored in this space? Does every item fit me well and flatter my appearance and style? Is every item in proper working order (no holes or other damage)? Is there any item I've been holding on to that makes me sad or frustrated?*

30 SECONDS

❏ Remove one item of clothing you haven't worn in more than a year or that you dislike. Put it in a bag to donate to charity.

❏ Straighten any clothing that isn't hanging properly on its hanger.

❏ Remove unused hangers from in between clothes and store them on a hanger organizer or at one end of the clothing rod.

❏ Arrange hangers so that pants are with pants, dress shirts are with dress shirts, etc. Work in thirty-second increments. If organizing this way isn't your forte, arrange by what makes sense to you—season, outfit, color, etc. (Take the quiz on page 87 to determine how to best organize your clothes.)

❏ Arrange shoes by type—slippers, boots, sneakers, flats, heels, etc. Work in thirty-second increments.

1 MINUTE

❏ Pull out any items that need mending (broken zippers, torn hems) and put them in a bag to take to the tailor. If you want to repair the item yourself, write a note and attach it to the bag with a date two weeks from now—if you haven't repaired the item by then, take it to the tailor or consider getting rid of it.

❏ Return shoes to their shoe rack, cubby, or boxes.

❏ Inspect belts, scarves, and ties for damage and straighten them to avoid kinks and wrinkles.

❏ Gather up and dispose of any trash—dry cleaner bags and tags, plastic tagging fasteners and price tags, damaged hangers, etc.

❏ Remove one item of clothing that you don't believe fits you well or properly. Try it on and study yourself in a mirror or take a picture of yourself with your smartphone, and be extremely honest with yourself as to whether it flatters you. If it doesn't, put it in a bag to donate to charity.

5 MINUTES

❏ Install a hook, basket, or bin so you have an official place to put "clerty" clothes (not clean, not dirty), like previously worn jeans and sweaters.

❏ Actually *clean* your closet. Vacuum or sweep the floor of the closet and corners of the ceiling. Who knows what you'll find? Maybe that scarf or tie you thought you'd lost.

❏ If you keep a hamper in your closet, scoop it up and start a load of laundry or get it ready to go to the laundromat.

❏ Install adhesive LED tap lights in different areas of your closet if you need better lighting to see your things. Don't let your clothes and potential clutter hide in the dark.

❏ Set up your iron and/or steamer and get the wrinkles out of a piece of clean-yet-rumpled clothing hanging in your closet. Everything in your closet should be *prêt-à-porter* (that's French for "ready-to-wear").

15 MINUTES

❏ Polish a couple of pairs of leather shoes and inspect their soles for damage. If necessary, take shoes in need of repair to a cobbler.

❏ Feeling frustrated with what your wardrobe has to offer? Instead of going shopping, invite a trusted friend over to help you create new outfits with what you already own. Pull out your accessories and shoes and see how you can spice up your current collection. You may find that one or two new pieces of clothing or new accessories might really be beneficial, but most likely you'll be satisfied with what you have.

❏ Make rules for your wardrobe regarding future purchases. Examples: Don't buy any item of clothing unless it's *exactly* what you want. Don't buy any item of clothing that doesn't fit you properly the moment you're buying it (maternity clothing is the exception to this rule). Don't buy any item of clothing that doesn't work with at least three other pieces in your wardrobe.

❏ Try on all your shoes. Get rid of any that cause blisters, don't fit you well, or that you no longer love or want.

❏ Donate a full bag of clothing (or two) to a local charity.

HANGERS THAT HANG AROUND

Hangers seem to breed like rabbits. Even expensive wood or flocked hangers seem to appear out of nowhere and take over clothes and coat closets. So, how many do you realistically need, and what do you do with the extras? I'll admit it, I'm a bit of a hanger snob. Since I don't have many clothes, I invest a great deal of attention in the care of what I do have. That means I like my hangers to help my clothes keep their shape instead of destroying them, so I buy fancy ones. I currently have ten hangers more than items in my foyer's coat closet so guests have somewhere to hang their coats when they visit. In my personal closet, I have just five extra hangers. All metal hangers from the dry cleaner are kept at the end of the rod, and I take them back to the dry cleaners to be recycled whenever I drop off clothing.

Having only five extra hangers keeps me committed to the one-in, one-out rule for clothes acquisition, but still gives me a little leeway. Can you reduce your hanger collection to help keep clutter at bay in your closets?

QUIZ

How to Organize Your Closet

Is your current closet organizing system not working for you? Take this quiz and then look at your results to find advice on how to make your closet work for your needs and preferences. Choose the answer that generally describes you.

1. **How do you organize books on your bookshelf?**
   A. By author, title, or subject
   B. By spine color or book size
   C. I don't

2. **How do you organize your to-do list?**
   A. Actions grouped by projects
   B. By where I can complete the task
   C. I don't, it's just one massive list
   D. I don't have a to-do list

3. **If you put a piece of paper in a file and stick it in a filing cabinet, do you:**
   A. Instantly forget the paper exists
   B. Remember you have the paper and reference it as necessary
   C. Never put the piece of paper in the file
   D. Stick it in a catchall file that isn't labeled but you can search through if needed

4. **How many receipts are there currently in your purse/wallet/pocket?**
   A. None, I don't buy anything
   B. None, I scan and file them each time I come home
   C. A few, I clean out my purse/wallet/pockets about once a week
   D. There are so many crumpled in there, I don't even want to count; or I throw them away immediately and hope I never have to dispute an inaccuracy

5. **How often do you floss your teeth?**
   - A. Daily, sometimes twice daily
   - B. A few times a week
   - C. Only right before my dentist appointments, if then
   - D. Only when something gets stuck in my teeth

SCORING:

1. a. 1, b. 5, c. 15
2. a. 1, b. 5, c. 10, d. 15
3. a. 5, b. 1, c. 15, d. 10
4. a. 5, b. 1, c. 10, d. 15
5. a. 1, b. 5, c. 15, d. 10

RESULTS:

< 20 POINTS   *You're super organized and your closet probably already looks fabulous.* You follow through on your actions, so a highly organized solution could easily work for you.

CLOSET-ORGANIZING STYLES TO TRY:

· By type of clothes (all short-sleeve shirts grouped together, all dress slacks together) and then by color within each group (lightest to darkest or vice versa)
· By outfit (all the coordinating pieces of a suit together)

21–40 POINTS   *You are likely a highly visual person.* When your closet has a lot of space between clothes on hangers, you can see outfit combinations better and imagine yourself wearing the clothes. Don't cram too many clothes into your closet or you will constantly be trying on outfits to "see" them.

CLOSET-ORGANIZING STYLES TO TRY:

· By color (it will give you a great amount of pleasure each time you open your closet)

· Hang a valet rod in your closet or a hook on the back of your closet door so you can pull out potential outfits to see them better.

41-60 POINTS *You're probably easygoing and have minimalist tendencies.* The fewer clothes you have, the less laundry you have to do, and the less time you have to spend hanging up clothes. If you have a lot of clothes, downsizing will help you immensely, since putting in the time to keep everything organized isn't really for you.

CLOSET-ORGANIZING STYLES TO TRY:

· By season. Keep it simple and have all your summer stuff in one section and your winter stuff in another. Jeans can be the great dividing line between the two.
· By outfit. Use cubbies instead of a clothing rod. A giant dresser for most of your clothes would probably work well for you.

> 60 POINTS *You're likely overwhelmed and your clothes might live in laundry baskets most of the time.* This is a stressful habit you will want to break if it applies to you. The reasons your clothes likely live in laundry baskets are varied, but one major reason might be that you have more clothes than you have space to adequately store them. A solid uncluttering can be helpful, and so will a trusted accountability partner to help you weed out the clutter and keep the gems in your closet.

CLOSET-ORGANIZING STYLES TO TRY:

· Don't think about organizing styles just yet. First spend the next couple of months doing your best to get your clothes onto hangers in your closet and folded in your dresser immediately after you do a load of laundry. Once you're set in this routine, check out the tips for the score between 41 and 60 points for suggestions.

Fashion Forward

It doesn't take a lot of clothing to have an incredible wardrobe. It's about quality—what fits you well, flatters your body, and makes you feel confident—not quantity. Having a lot of clothes you don't wear or don't want to wear isn't doing you any favors except for taking up room in your home. Clearing the clutter from your closet and working to keep it out will save you time, money, and energy in your busy life.

WHAT YOU'LL NEED: A bag, box, or bin to hold clothes and shoes you wish to donate to charity, a pair of scissors, a full-length mirror, and a trash can. You may also want a friend or family member you respect to work with you.

UNCLUTTER YOUR CLOSET!

1. **ROUND UP WHAT YOU OWN.** Coats, formal wear, garden shoes, belts, scarves, seasonal clothes—bring it all together. Everything should be clean so it's ready to be donated if that is the choice you ultimately make for a piece of clothing.

2. **GROUP LIKE ITEMS WITH LIKE ITEMS.** Get all your sweaters together in one spot and all your socks in another. It's easier to work when you know exactly how much of one type of clothing you have.

3. **GET RID OF THE OBVIOUS CLUTTER.** Grab anything you immediately know should go into the donation bag, the rag pile, or the trash, and put it there. You can do this while you're grouping things together if you wish to save time.

4. **IDENTIFY DUPLICATES.** Based on your style, having duplicates of some items may be what you desire (I work from home, so I have four pairs of jeans—when I worked in a traditional office, I had three pairs of black pants). However, not everyone needs multiples of some items, and some of the multiples you own may not actually be in rotation. Look at all of them and decide if any can go.

5. **PART WITH THE OLD AND DECREPIT.** If you have a T-shirt from college and you've been out of college for fifteen years, it's time to let that old T-shirt go. You could have it made into a quilt of old T-shirts if you wish to hang on to it for sentimental reasons, but you don't need to keep wearing it. The fibers in clothes break down over time, and if you wear something regularly it will start showing signs of decomposition after many years. The item is likely more qualified for the rag pile than for you to wear it.

6. **GET RID OF WHAT YOU DON'T WEAR.** If you haven't worn something in ages, let it go. It's unlikely situations will change and you'll start wearing the item. Some people get rid of things if they haven't worn them in a season, others in a year. There isn't necessarily a set period of time—you know what you don't wear, so get rid of it.

7. **EVALUATE WHAT IS LEFT.** Try items on and pay attention to how you feel about them. Does the piece of clothing flatter you? Does it fit you? Does it elicit compliments from others or give you confidence? Is it your style? Does it project the image you wish it to? Remember: A piece of clothing that doesn't flatter or fit you well can accentuate the parts of your body that you may not wish to emphasize. Only keep clothing that looks best on you. Let go of any item that doesn't fit you, flatter you, and make you feel confident right now.

8. **ASK A FRIEND TO PURGE TWO ITEMS.** We all have items we love that we *think* look awesome on us . . . but may not actually be doing us any favors. Once a year, I ask my husband if there are any items of clothing he hates that I wear all the time. If he does, I give those pieces to charity. Then I pluck two pieces from his wardrobe that I don't like and call it even. Some years we don't find anything to purge and other years we wish we had more than two choices. You can obviously skip this step, but it's a strategy you may want to try.

9. **PUT IT ALL BACK.** When returning clothes to your closet and dresser, put the clothes back in an organized manner. Have all clothing facing the same direction and group it in the way that makes the most sense to you. I prefer to organize by type (all short-sleeve shirts together, all long-sleeve shirts

together, all skirts, all pants, etc.) and then by color within the type (darkest color on the left continuing to lightest color on the right). Other people may prefer to organize by outfits or only by color. Take the quiz on page 87 and use the system that makes the most sense to you. Also, remember these four tips that work in almost any closet:

- **LEAVE SPACE BETWEEN HANGERS.** In the closet, leave room so you can slide the hangers easily on the clothing rod. Based on how much space you have, this may mean you need to do some more purging. But if you can't easily see your clothes, you may forget you have them or they may sustain damage without your being aware of it.

- **USE QUALITY HANGERS.** You don't want clothes creasing, puckering, or sliding onto the floor, so use quality hangers. I have three types of hangers in my closet for different items: suit coats, pants, and everything else. For most items, I like the narrow, space-saving hangers with flocking so light fabrics have something to hold on to and don't fall to the floor.

- **CONSIDER USING CLOTHING ROD DIVIDERS.** If you're an extremely visual person, consider using clothing rod dividers (those white plastic rings you see in clothing stores) to separate areas of your closet. Use a label maker to label the tag. This is a great trick for children's closets when you may have clothes of different sizes or purpose (school clothes, play clothes).

- **INSTALL A VALET ROD ON YOUR CLOSET DOOR.** I prefer to save time in the morning by choosing my clothes the night before (it's part of my before-bed routine—see page 239). A valet rod or a hook on the back of your closet door can help you see all the parts of your outfit and set them aside so you won't have to rush.

10. **DONATE PURGED CLOTHES TO CHARITY.** Take the clothes to a donation center as quickly as possible so they don't continue to clutter up your home.

Nursery and Young Children's Bedrooms

From diapers to toys to carriers to tiny shoes, you can easily feel overwhelmed by all the new things you now have to care for—in addition to the little bundle of joy who has graced your life. In addition to giving feedings and changing diapers, you also want to nurture and teach this child how to care for and respect her things as she grows. This room is an opportunity for achieving just that objective. You'll come and go from this space more regularly than an older child's room, so it has to meet both your needs and your child's. With a little work and some ingenuity, you can achieve all of your goals for this space.

When working in this area, ask yourself: *Are items in this space organized in a way that is convenient for teaching my child independent organizing skills? Is this area free of clutter so as to promote good sleep habits for my child? Is this area free of clutter so as to ensure the child's safety?*

30 SECONDS

- ❏ Lie on your belly, scan the floor, and pick up any small items that could be choking hazards.

- ❏ Straighten diapers, wipes, and any other supplies that might be disorderly. Dispose of any trash.

- ❏ Empty the diaper pail.

❏ Replace any safety items, like electrical plug covers, that may have been temporarily removed.

❏ Put away anything that has been set on the rocking chair.

1 MINUTE

❏ Straighten and/or return books to shelves.

❏ Gather stuffed animals and toys together and place them in the toy bin or toy area.

❏ Inspect the crib and other furniture in the room for damage and safety concerns. Schedule time on your calendar to fix any problems you discover.

❏ Check levels on supplies: diapers, wipes, diaper pail bags, etc. Add items that are low to your shopping list.

❏ Make the bed: Pull everything out of a crib or make up a toddler's/ young child's bed.

5 MINUTES

❏ Vacuum the rocking chair, the ottoman, and the underside of the crib.

❏ Using a yardstick or other long, narrow item, sweep out any objects that may have fallen under large pieces of furniture and put those items away.

❏ Open a clothing drawer/closet and pull out any clothing that is too small. Put these items in a bag to be donated to charity.

❏ Likely not kept *in* your child's room, but in the same vein, wipe down the seat of his/her stroller.

❏ Again, you don't keep your child's high chair in his/her room, but since it relates to your youngster, give the chair a thorough cleaning. If the high chair has a cloth cover, you may wish to detach it and throw it in the washing machine.

15 MINUTES

❏ Label clothing rod dividers to identify sizes of clothing, and then sort hanging clothes by size.

❏ Label dresser drawers and toy boxes and bins with pictures and simple words (pajamas, shirts, trains, stuffed animals) so children can begin to identify how their clothes and toys are organized.

❏ Your child's car seat isn't located in his/her room, but now is a good time to vacuum out the seat and wipe down its straps.

❏ Lower a closet rod or install a closet doubler rod so children can begin to access their hanging clothes.

❏ Hang a closet sweater organizer so children can have a place in their closet or dresser to place the clothing you or they have chosen for the next day.

Teaching Children Organizing, Uncluttering, and Cleaning Skills

Children are fantastic at making messes. But, thankfully, you can help them build a solid foundation of cleaning, uncluttering, and organizing skills to take care of the messes they create. Learning these useful skills early in life will help children keep their stress in check, fight clutter before it becomes a burden, and build strong time-management skills that will aid them in the classroom and when they move out into the world. Here are some general skills you might wish to teach at each developmental stage.

YOUNG CHILDREN (FIFTEEN MONTHS TO FOUR YEARS): Pick up after yourself to model cleaning and organizing behaviors for your child. Demonstrate and aid your child when he needs to pick up his toys at the end of every play period and before bedtime. In addition to any floor cleaning you do, your child can use a small hand broom and dustpan to sweep up large pieces of dry food that fall on the floor during mealtimes. She can help to wipe down the tray of her high chair with a wet sponge after you clean up the really messy stuff. He can throw away trash with your guidance. She can put dirty clothes in a clothes hamper. With all of these tasks, it's the habit of cleaning up immediately after an activity that is most important, not the effectiveness of the task.

ELEMENTARY SCHOOL–AGE CHILDREN (FIVE TO TEN YEARS): Younger children will need assistance, but eventually the goal is to transition yourself into an advisory role by the time your child is in fifth grade. Chores may include making his bed, picking clothes to wear to school the next day, setting the table, clearing and cleaning the table, loading the dishwasher, unloading and putting away clean silverware, sorting her laundry into lights and darks, feeding pets, hanging up his coat upon entering the home, sweeping and vacuuming, dusting, picking up toys in a room, selecting which school papers to keep in a scrapbook or portfolio and which ones to dispose of/recycle, and putting away toys, games, equipment, homework, etc., after use. By age ten, most children are perfectly capable of doing all these activities. Again, it's the habit development that is most important.

MIDDLE SCHOOL–AGE CHILDREN (ELEVEN TO THIRTEEN YEARS): You'll still need to advise your child in these activities, but likely less guidance will be required than in previous years. Chores may include washing his clothes, choosing clothes from her closet that no longer fit and can be donated to charity, changing the sheets on his bed, washing interior windows, cleaning electronics (keyboards, television screens), washing the car, vacuuming the interior of the car, shoveling snow, sweeping sidewalks and the driveway, sweeping porches and the front steps, walking the dog and changing kitty litter boxes, cleaning bathtubs and toilets, as well as the chores listed for younger children.

HIGH SCHOOL–AGE CHILDREN (FOURTEEN TO EIGHTEEN YEARS): By this age, most children will be able to fully participate in completing chores around the home. In addition to what has been previously mentioned, this may include helping plan and cook meals, packing her lunches, mowing the yard, babysitting younger siblings, and other activities. At this stage, you can demonstrate how to complete the chores a few times, but after that expect chores to be completed satisfactorily without your advising (but certainly with your stated appreciation).

Preteens' and Teenagers' Bedrooms

Older children have the ability to take on the tasks of organizing, cleaning, and uncluttering their bedrooms, but some still want or need assistance. Since you know your child best, feel welcome to hand over this book directly to him or work through it together, based on his abilities. Whatever you do, don't invade the space without your child present. This would do far more damage to your relationship than a messy room might do to your home.

When working in this area, ask yourself: *How can I work with my child to better organize and unclutter her room while still giving her privacy and respecting her boundaries? Is there an obvious place where I can recommend help—a new clothes hamper or an organizer for his video game equipment— that won't come across as judgmental? What words can I use that are supportive and helpful?*

30 SECONDS

❏ Make the bed.

❏ Straighten clothes in the dresser and closet, moving all empty hangers to one end of the rod or to a hanger organizer.

❏ Put dirty clothes and towels into the hamper.

❏ Put desk items away.

❏ Clean a mirror, dust a shelf, or complete any quick cleaning task that you have avoided for too long.

1 MINUTE

❏ Put away clean clothes or straighten clothes in drawers.

❏ Pull out any items that have fallen behind or under the bed or dresser and put them away.

❏ Take any food items and/or dirty dishes to the kitchen.

❏ Straighten books on a bookshelf.

❏ Return anything in the room that isn't yours to its rightful owner.

5 MINUTES

❏ Sort through clothes and shoes and put any that are too small into a box to be passed along to a younger sibling or donated to charity.

❏ Sort through sock and underwear drawers and pull out any garments that have holes, stains, or damaged elastic. Throw them away or recycle by adding to the rag pile.

❏ Change the bedsheets and remake the bed.

❏ Look at books and/or toys and select at least one (or more) that can be passed along to a younger sibling or donated to charity.

❏ Clear off flat surfaces and return misplaced items to their proper locations.

15 MINUTES

❏ Clean out desk drawers and get rid of clutter. When putting items away, organize them so that the supplies you need the most often are easiest to access. Group similar objects together.

DIY TIP:
CREATE A DESK DRAWER ORGANIZER

Collect leftover cereal, checkbook, and stationery boxes, cut them down to the height of your desk drawer, and cover them in washi tape to create your very own desk drawer organizer to help keep items in place. Label each section so you know where to find and return items.

❏ Organize clothes in the closet so that pants are with pants and shirts are with shirts and all clothes are facing the same direction. You could also group by outfit. (See page 88 for more closet organizing styles.) Whatever method you use, keep some space around each item of clothing so it's easy to see and access.

❏ Wash any mattress or pillow covers from your bed. You should also wash your pillow every few months. Rotate and/or flip your mattress if it is recommended for the type of mattress you have. Remake the bed when everything is clean.

❑ If you have a jewelry box, straighten up the contents. Match earrings to ensure you're not missing any and then group all your earrings together. Untangle necklaces and bracelets. Check rings to make sure stones or designs aren't loose and at risk of falling off. If any of the jewelry is too small for you to wear, discuss with a parent what you should do with it.

❑ Is there an adult in your life who is begging you to clean your room? Be honest: Could your room actually use a thorough deep cleaning? If so, give the room the attention it deserves. Vacuum/sweep floors in the room and closet, wipe down doorknobs, vacuum air vents, replace filters in humidifiers or air purifiers, clean out under the bed, dust ceiling fans and all surfaces, and wipe down baseboards, light switches, and electrical plates.

Home Office

Maintaining a home requires time and attention, and completing these responsibilities also requires a little bit of space. You may use your home office only to pay bills and keep track of your personal calendar, or you may use it daily for your job. Regardless of your specific needs, it's essential that you have a space and appropriate tools to support you in these endeavors.

When working in this area, ask yourself: *Is this space organized in such a way as to make doing work at home enjoyable and efficient? Is my desk free of clutter that might distract me from my most important tasks? If I share this area, is it set up so multiple people can work without diminishing each other's productivity? Do I have all the tools I need, and are those tools working properly?*

30 SECONDS

❏ Gather wayward writing utensils or paper clips and put them into their designated container.

❏ Copy important information off a single sticky note and put that information someplace safe and more permanent (like on your calendar or to-do list if it's a task or event, or into your contacts if it's a phone number, etc.—wherever the information really belongs).

❏ Take any food items (mugs, plates, cans, spoons, snacks) back to the kitchen for washing or storage.

❏ Close tabs or programs not currently in use on the computer.

❏ Throw away any trash not currently in the trash can.

1 MINUTE

❏ Wipe down your phone, keyboard, mouse, and computer monitor with cleaner that is appropriate for these devices.

❏ Restock paper in your printer.

❏ Straighten books on the bookshelf.

❏ Empty the trash can and wipe off any stuck-on items with a disinfecting wipe.

❏ Adjust the height of your desk chair (if you use a sitting desk) so you can work with proper posture. Make other adjustments to your desk height, computer keyboard, and other items to achieve good ergonomics.

5 MINUTES

❏ Rearrange items on your desk so that the things you need most often are the easiest to reach and the things you only sometimes need are stored in containers, in drawers, or on shelves.

❏ If you share this space with children or a spouse/partner/roommate, identify what materials will be shared and what materials will be personal.

❏ Remove any items from this space that do not help you to take care of your responsibilities to your home and/or your job. Return those items to their appropriate storage locations.

❏ Arrange reference books/materials you regularly access in the way that makes the most sense to you, ensuring that pulling one item out doesn't destroy the entire system or knock it over.

❏ Check off items you've already completed from your to-do list (see "Four Steps to Creating an Effective To-Do List" on page 111) or write down as many tasks as you can think of that you need to do. Set a timer so you don't go over five minutes.

15 MINUTES

❏ Set a timer for fifteen minutes and process/file as many items as you can from your physical inbox in that time.

❏ Label both ends of power and connection cables so it is easy to identify which device each cord belongs to. (See page 28 for more cable-related suggestions.)

❏ Dust. Then, using a handheld vacuum, clean the dust bunnies out from under all your furniture, the wheels of your desk chair, and around your surge protector/power strip.

❏ Do the annoying item on your to-do list that has been languishing for way too long but that won't take you very long. Just buck up and do it.

❏ Sort through the contents of your supply closet or drawer and inventory what you currently have. Organize the items so like items are together and no pile of items is at risk of tipping over. If you have more supplies of a certain kind than you could ever imagine using (especially supplies related to technology you no longer use, like toner for an old printer), consider selling them on eBay or donating them to a charity that could use them. Test pens and markers to ensure they still work and toss any that don't.

There is a cost involved with the following tip, but you might find it extremely beneficial: Purchase duplicate charging cables and adapters for your electronics. Having more than one cable prevents having to continually shuffle cables between your house, car, and office (and possibly losing them in the process). You'll never be caught without the cable you need, and you'll save yourself time unplugging and replugging cables.

FOUR STEPS TO CREATING AN EFFECTIVE TO-DO LIST

1. **WRITE IT DOWN OR TYPE IT UP.** The reasoning behind this tip is so glaringly obvious that I almost didn't mention it. Simply get the stuff in your head onto your written or digital to-do list so it's no longer just floating around in your brain.

2. **BREAK IT DOWN.** Vague items on your list like "lose weight" will never get completed. They're overwhelming. Figure out exactly the steps you need to take to lose the weight or write the book or call your mom more often, and put those actions on your list.

3. **SCHEDULE IT.** When an action you need to take makes it onto your to-do list, it should also make it onto your calendar. You need to call Shannon? Schedule a time to make that call. Make your kid a costume for the school play? Schedule an hour on your calendar each day this week to work on the costume. If you don't schedule the time, the task runs the risk of not being completed.

4. **BE REALISTIC.** You don't have superpowers, so don't create a to-do list that supposes you have them. Be honest about how much time it takes to complete tasks, what kind of energy levels you have, and if you will be able to complete the task at the time of day you think you will, and don't put things on your list that you won't actually do. If someone else (a boss or supervisor) is asking too much of you, sit down with him/her and work out a plan and schedule that can actually be accomplished. I'm giving you permission right now to ask for help.

Create Your Ideal Home Office

The place where you take care of the business of your home and personal life should be a comfortable, motivating, and productive place to work. Whether you only have room for a desk in your bedroom or you have an entire office with a door doesn't matter—your home office space can be uncluttered, organized, clean, and inviting.

WHAT YOU'LL NEED: A pad of paper and a pen so you can record to-do items and reminders; a cardboard box where you can temporarily store papers, materials, or notes; a trash can, recycling bin, shredder, and donation bin.

GET TO WORK!

When organizing your home office, keep these three questions at the forefront of your mind:

1. Is this item related to taking care of my responsibilities?
2. Does this object meet my needs and support my work, and do I fully understand how to use it?
3. Does this object work? (Does the pen have ink? Does the scanner scan?)

If you come upon an object that doesn't elicit a "yes" to either of the first two questions, it's quite possible the object is clutter or simply doesn't belong in your home office space. Purge it or find a better home for it. If the answer to question 3 is "no," even if it meets the requirements of the first two questions, get rid of it or have it repaired right now.

Methodically work through your office in sections. I like to think of the area as a clockface (with the computer keyboard as 12 o'clock) and begin with 12 to 2, then 2 to 4, 4 to 6, 6 to 8, 8 to 10, and finally 10 to 12. Working this way keeps you focused on a small area and helps reduce distractions.

Common sense is really the best tool you can use when organizing your office. If you have to lean over to reach the phone each time it rings, arrange your desk so your phone is closer to your chair or get a hands-free headset so all you have to do is touch a button on the headset to answer a call. If you keep grabbing pens from your pen cup that don't work, test them all and throw out the duds. Store things in places that make sense and remember to have a place for everything. Reams of paper should be stored with other reams of paper near your printer, and books with other books on a bookshelf.

Shelving is always a good storage idea in an office space because shelves put the walls to work for you. If you need more of a work surface, walls can be used for bulletin boards or painted with chalkboard or magnetic paint. You can even use a magnetic primer and then put chalkboard paint over the top so you get the benefits of both.

ADDITIONAL HELP: To learn more about uncluttering and organizing your papers, see page 198. If your computer itself is causing you stress, turn to page 205. If cables are giving you a headache, page 28 can help alleviate that pain.

FINAL NOTE: Charities are often in need of office supplies, so if you're not using a product, there might be a group out there that would really appreciate it.

CAN AN APP DO THAT?

Over the years, you've likely said good-bye to numerous pieces of office hardware and supplies because technology has advanced in such a way that the device or material has become obsolete. If you own a computer and/or smartphone, you may be able to ditch or avoid acquiring new office items and simply download an app instead.

Things you may not realize a computer and/or smartphone app can do for you:

TASK	APP	HOW IT HELPS
To-do lists	Todoist	Captures tasks you need to do and creates games to motivate you to complete chores
Scanning	Evernote, ScanWritr, or CamCard	A scan is an image, same as a picture. These apps let you take an image with the camera on your smartphone and then save it to the app.
Manage photographs	iPhoto, Aperture, Lightroom, Flickr, Google Photos, and dozens of others	Lets you label individuals in images, identify where the picture was taken with GPS coordinates, arrange images into albums, and numerous other organizing functions

TASK	APP	HOW IT HELPS
Sign documents	EchoSign	Lets you (almost always legally) sign and digitally process a document
Fax	Acrobat Reader and your e-mail program	Turns a document into a PDF to be e-mailed
Voice messages to text	YouMail	Translates voice mails into typed messages and e-mails them to you
Photocopying	FedEx Mobile	Sends a document directly to your local FedEx Office, where you can pick it up when it's convenient for you

Pantry and Food

Food is essential for survival, yet your pantry may not reflect this truly important aspect of your life. Instead of supporting you in your nutritional endeavors, it may work against you if it is cluttered, disorganized, and/or filled with food you don't want or shouldn't eat. A well-organized and well-maintained pantry can enrich your life in the most basic of ways, and a weekly meal plan can remove the problem of wondering what's for dinner.

When working in this area, ask yourself: *What items am I missing? What items are expired and simply taking up space? Does my pantry promote healthy eating habits? Do I have a simple way to create a shopping list and a scheduled time each week to create a meal plan? Is food organized in such a way that everyone who uses this area is able to find what they need? If eating at home is a priority, does this space help me to reach that goal?*

30 SECONDS

❑ Check the expiration/use-by dates on a few items in your pantry and dispose of any that are no longer safe to consume (reference the date stamped on the product by the manufacturer and/or StillTasty.com if you have any questions). Check as many items as you can in thirty seconds. Repeat until your entire pantry has been checked.

❑ Gather any food you will not or do not wish to eat by its expiration date and put it in a box or bag to take to charity.

❑ Straighten cans and/or boxes of food items.

- ❏ Gather up spice and sauce packets and put them in a small box or bin.

- ❏ Sweep the floor.

1 MINUTE

- ❏ Collect your reusable shopping bags and put them in your hamper to be laundered.

- ❏ Grab a rag or paper towel and pull the gunk off the bottom of your kitchen broom.

- ❏ Turn containers so it's easy to see labels or identify interior contents.

- ❏ Put plastic bags inside a larger plastic bag to prepare them for recycling.

- ❏ Keep a few paper bags for errands but put all the rest in the recycling bin.

5 MINUTES

- ❏ Group like items together, either in shallow bins or in proximity on shelves. Label the bin or shelf to make it apparent where things belong. Groupings might be: pasta, flours, cereals, spices, dried herbs, snacks, etc.

- ❏ Review any small appliances or other nonfood items to see if there are any you haven't used in years or that might need to be repaired or cleaned.

❏ Move any chemical cleaners (bleach, ammonia, etc.) to a utility closet for safety.

❏ Pull items off a shelf, wipe down the shelf, and return the items.

❏ Flip through a cookbook and find a meal idea that uses items you already have in your pantry.

15 MINUTES

❏ Create a list of pantry staples you regularly use in your kitchen. (There are many lists online that you can customize to your needs.) Laminate the list or digitize it so you can mark items when you run out, as well as refer to it each time you put together a meal plan or shopping list.

❏ Consider installing a motion-sensor light in this space. Since you often come to or leave the pantry with full hands, it is nice to have an automatic light.

❏ Take any food items to be donated to charity to that charity.

❏ Bring plastic bags to a grocery store for recycling.

❏ Refill containers—salt into the salt shaker, pepper into the pepper mill, sugar into the sugar bowl, etc.

Need dinner inspiration? Check out the meal planning advice on the next page or look on page 251 for when your family is hungry and you're out of ideas.

Meal Planning and the Family Meal

I'm a huge proponent of the family meal. My preference is for the people I love to come together at the kitchen table for good food and conversation at breakfast and dinner. There is a solid amount of research out there that reveals that kids who eat family meals at home (with the television off) tend to get better grades, have fewer issues with peer pressure and drugs, and feel more connected to their families. Meals cooked at home are also usually more healthful than meals consumed in restaurants or from drive-through windows. However, I'm also a pragmatic person who works full-time and is part of an active family. This means my ideal preferences and reality don't always align, as I'm sure is the case for most American families.

Instead of feeling guilty for not meeting my ideal preference 100 percent of the time, I've come to embrace a standard I call the *pragmatic ideal*. This means that a meal I dumped into the slow cooker that cooked all day long unassisted is as good as a meal I labored over for hours. It also means that sometimes the family eats together at a restaurant—a sit-down place where the kids can practice their manners and someone other than me can do the dishes. Pragmatic ideal means that sometimes the grocery store roasts the chicken and I carve it up, or that the fillet of tilapia was frozen before I threw it under the broiler. It also means that instead of fresh vegetables bought at a farmers' market, I might be steaming frozen vegetables in the microwave. It means that every Tuesday is taco night because everybody loves taco night.

If having family meals is your preference, you're more likely to make them happen when the meals are easy and don't stress you out. Save your mealtime anxiety for when you're entertaining the queen. Create weekly meal plans that are right for you and your family and that meet *your* pragmatic ideal.

HOW TO CREATE A MEAL PLAN

The two most common ways to create a weekly meal plan are to do it using an app, like Plan to Eat, or using pen and paper. I use both, based on my mood.

Irrespective of the method you choose, consider the following tips for making meal planning a breeze:

· Set a time to meal plan as part of your weekly routine. For example, I plan meals for the upcoming week every Saturday morning while I'm drinking my morning coffee.

· Schedule two trips to the grocery store each week (such as a big trip on Saturday morning and a quick trip on Wednesday after work). Doing this will allow you to have fresh produce and meat the second half of the week.

· If you have multiple people in your home over the age of fifteen, share the cooking responsibilities by assigning days (Sally = Mondays, Wednesdays. Tom = Tuesdays, Thursdays. Bob = Saturdays).

· Have a regular repetition of favorite meals. For your home, this might mean every Tuesday is taco night. Or create a thirty-day meal plan everyone enjoys and then repeat it for a series of months.

· Pull out your cookbooks or recipes you've favorited on

cooking sites and Pinterest, and use them for inspiration. If you don't do it now, when will you ever make these potentially wonderful meals? Donate or sell any cookbooks you don't plan to use.

· When creating your grocery shopping list, organize it based on where items are located in your grocery store to save yourself time. (If you keep your shopping list digitally, apps like Paprika have this functionality.)

Knife Skills and *Mise en Place*

Of everything I've learned about cooking, there are two things that I believe have helped me the most. The first: knife skills. The second: *mise en place.*

Whether you are a quality home cook or a novice, I highly recommend taking a knife skills course through a local culinary school (almost all offer courses for home cooks in addition to their student programs). Be sure to take a class that involves hands-on instruction (avoid demonstration-only classes). If the school offers intermediate and advanced knife skills classes, I recommend taking them, too. Having good knife skills improves your speed in the kitchen, reduces the likelihood of accidents, and reduces the number of specialty gadgets you might be tempted to buy.

Mise en place is one of those concepts I thought was completely unnecessary until six years ago. (That's when I became a mother and mealtimes became much more hectic in our home.) If you're unfamiliar with the term, it's French for "set in place" or "put in place." In practice, it is the act of clearing your workspace before you begin, pulling out any utensils or cooking implements you'll need, measuring and preparing all ingredients, setting the prepared ingredients in order of use, cooking, and then cleaning the workspace after you have cooked. It's the cooking equivalent of "a place for everything and everything in its place."

Although it might sound counterintuitive, cooking in this manner and having all your ingredients prepared ahead of time actually saves you time (by being ready with ingredients at the exact moment you need them) and money (because you ruin fewer meals and waste fewer ingredients). If you have children, it also provides you with an opportunity to have them help you prepare ingredients for the meal and not have to worry about them getting too close to a heat source.

When cooking, this is usually how I approach it:

1. Read through a recipe.
2. Read through the recipe a second time, this time making notes about any new techniques or tricky timing combinations.
3. Clear and prepare all work surfaces.
4. If necessary, preheat the oven.
5. Set the table.
6. Gather all ingredients and supplies.
7. Measure all ingredients.
8. Put away all unused ingredients, such as the large container of flour from which you measured, in the pantry.
9. Organize ingredients and supplies in order of use, as directed by the recipe.
10. Cook.
11. Put dirtied items into the dishwasher as time permits while cooking.
12. Eat.
13. Clean the kitchen and dining room so they're ready to be used for the next meal.

Hobby Workspace

Whether it's woodworking, sketching, painting, building robots, rebuilding engines, knitting, playing sports, restoring antiques, sewing, tracking your fantasy football team, or researching your family's genealogy, your favorite hobby or hobbies likely take up physical space in your home. Keeping these items in order ultimately allows you more time to enjoy your hobby and experience it more fully.

When working in this area, ask yourself: *Do I make time to actually participate in this hobby, and do I really enjoy it? Do I have more supplies stashed than I will ever be able to use in my lifetime? Are the items in this space organized safely and in such a way that others can access supplies easily?*

30 SECONDS

❏ Throw out scraps, shreds, or any small bits of material that you cannot currently think of using in a project.

❏ Unplug any equipment not currently in use to reduce chances of injury and your home's electrical consumption.

❏ Put away any wayward object in its proper storage location.

❏ Evaluate equipment to see if anything needs to be scheduled for maintenance, servicing, or replacement. If it does, see the follow-up project in the 15-minute section.

❏   Gather all supplies for a single project into a box, bin, or bag so every-thing is ready to go when you have time to work on it.

1 MINUTE

❏   Identify all your works in progress that need to be completed and set a date on your calendar to complete each of them.

❏   Schedule time on your calendar this week to devote to your hobby.

❏   Look at books or magazines you have for your hobby and pull out one or more you no longer need or want so you can sell or donate it (see 15-minute section).

❏   Wipe down/clean/dust any equipment or materials that need attention.

❏   Is there a project from the past that didn't go exactly as planned but that you could fix? If so, get the project and schedule time to fix it.

5 MINUTES

❏   Sort through some or all of your stash of materials and pull out anything you don't use to pass along to someone who will.

❏   Gather all small items—nails, pins, needles, clasps—from the bottoms of drawers or larger containers and group them together in a smaller container. Label the container so it's easy to find these small items in the future.

❏   Organize supplies in a drawer or cabinet so that the objects you need the most often are in the easiest-to-access locations.

❏ If you have any materials that could be damaged by pests, moisture, or temperature, move these materials to a container or location that reduces the risk of that type of damage.

❏ Track your progress and/or experiences with your hobby in a journal so you can see what changes you made to the instructions, comment on your satisfaction level with the project, and note if you would do it again. These notes will be valuable in the future when trying to decide on your next project or if someone comes to you for assistance with a similar project.

15 MINUTES

❏ List any books or magazines you no longer want or need for sale on a hobby-related website or similar method of sale.

❏ Take any materials you wish to donate to an appropriate group or charity (like wood you don't plan to use to a local school's woodshop program).

❏ Drop off any equipment that needs to be serviced at a repair shop that does the type of work you need completed.

❏ If you do not need to take an item to a repair shop to be serviced because you can do it yourself, complete the necessary work or schedule time on your calendar to do so.

❏ Research upcoming projects or opportunities to take on in the future and create a wish list. Set goals for skills you wish to master and how you hope to advance with your hobby. Check out websites like Meetup .com to see if there are others in your area with similar interests.

Wrap It Up!

You may be hiding your gift-wrapping supplies under a bed, in a closet, or in a dresser drawer. In many homes, these supplies are out of control and ready to burst. If this sounds like you, consider the following changes to your celebratory collection.

- **UNCLUTTER IT.** Group wrapping items you already own together by type and then sort through each of your piles and pull out anything that is damaged (that you will recycle or trash) or that you never anticipate using (that you can donate to a charity or friend).

- **CONTAIN IT.** If you don't already have a box, bin, or other container for your wrapping supplies, get one. It should be large enough to hold a few rolls of wrapping paper, some gift bags, bows, ribbons, tissue paper, clear tape, and scissors.

- **ORGANIZE IT.** Whatever you decide to keep, organize it in your storage container so that rolls of paper and bows aren't squished or damaged. Keep your groups together so that bows are stored next to bows and gift bags are stored next to gift bags.

- **SIMPLIFY.** After you use up the rolls of wrapping paper, tissue paper, and gift bags you already own, consider replacing them with silver papers and bags. Silver has the advantage of working for baby, birthday, wedding, graduation, anniversary, holiday, and no-reason-at-all gifts. If you have young children, a roll of plain white or brown paper also works well because you can easily decorate the bags or paper with drawings, stickers, and/or rubber stamps. You also can use a limited assortment of colored ribbons—blue, green, red, white—to further simplify your wrapping supplies.

· **MAKE IT WORK.** I'm not usually one to recommend having multiples of the same item, but when it comes to wrapping gifts, I make an exception. An extra pair of scissors and roll of clear tape to be stored with your wrapping supplies can save you time. That way, you don't have to hunt them down from somewhere else in the house when you want to wrap a gift, and you don't have to return them when you're done.

Stash Busting

One of my husband's hobbies is restoring vintage guitars and mandolins that are in rough shape. He gets the instruments at auctions, repairs them, and then resells them to people who will play them. Although he can make a little money in the process, it's mostly a labor of love. He hates seeing classic instruments wasting away, especially when a little attention is all they need to be great again. I think it's a fantastic hobby because it keeps instruments out of landfills, but on the downside, it also clutters up our home if he ends up with more instruments than he has the time to repair. Case in point: As I'm typing this, our daughter's room has two guitars in it, our bedroom has two, and the guitar rack in our living room (where he usually stores his projects) is packed full. It's time he sell off the ones that are already repaired, and cease acquiring more inventory even if it's a *good deal* until he can fit everything in the guitar rack. It's time for his stash to be busted.

Stash busting is the process of getting rid of excess supplies you no longer need, want, or can envision ever being able to use. Whether it's guitars, yarn, or pieces of lumber, a well-meant pile can quickly turn into a stash of clutter. With a little bit of time, some creative solutions, and a massive amount of willpower, you can get your stash under control.

WHAT YOU NEED: Time, creativity, and willpower

BUST THE STASH!

Give yourself a set amount of space to store your hobby's equipment and materials (for my husband, it's now the guitar rack in our living room and a shelf in the garage that holds shipping supplies).

Once that space is established, whittle your collection down to what you can store in that limited area. Deciding what to keep and what to purge is difficult, so you'll want to establish guidelines to help you make these decisions. These guidelines will vary by hobby, but you may choose to decide what to keep based on:

- value (only keep items worth more than X dollars)
- rarity (only items of which X number were ever made)
- likelihood of being used (I have a pattern for this yarn)
- most sentimental (treasured items given to me by loved ones)
- simply your favorites (love it)

Get rid of your excess stash. Sell it, donate it, or give it away—just get your materials down to a manageable amount of goods in a reasonable amount of time. If your hobby has an online enthusiasts' community, like Ravelry.com for knitters, start by listing your stash to see if there is someone who can put it to good use.

Places You Might Not Want to See

Linda Samuels, a professional organizer with Oh, So Organized! and past president of the Institute for Challenging Disorganization (ICD), on what one thing in her life cannot be in disarray:

We don't often consider our mind as being in "disarray." If I'm not clear about priorities for that week, day, or moment, everything becomes more challenging. My physical space can be completely organized, but without clear thinking, I'm more easily distracted, overwhelmed, and less productive. For me, organizing my thoughts and releasing extraneous mind clutter is essential.

Laundry Room

Of all the chores relating to the home, laundry seems to be the one that garners the most distaste. Putting some clothes in a washing machine isn't a difficult task, but once you involve carrying around hampers, sorting, folding, and putting clothes away, it's almost as if it is exercise instead of a hygienic act. The following tasks and a creation of a routine (be sure to check out the third task in the 15-minute section) will help you keep up with your laundry so that Mt. Laundry doesn't become a permanent mass in your home.

When working in this area, ask yourself: *Is there anything in this space that makes doing the laundry more difficult, like broken equipment or no place to easily fold clothes? Is this room inviting and well lit and somewhere I don't mind spending time? Are there things in this space that don't belong here? If I don't have a washer and dryer in my home, are there any problems with my system that make the process more of a hassle than necessary?*

30 SECONDS

❑　Clear the lint from the trap in the dryer.

❑　Wipe up any spills or lint or small messes that have accumulated on surfaces in the space and then put a placemat down under your supplies to make cleanup easier in the future.

❑　Check the washer's drainage tube/pipe to make sure it's not wiggling loose.

❑ Look behind the washer and dryer to see if anything has fallen behind them. Retrieve any items you find.

❑ Check the levels of your laundry supplies and add anything that is running low to your shopping list.

1 MINUTE

❑ Using a yardstick or broom handle, swipe out anything that has become wedged under the washer and dryer and any other pieces of furniture in the room.

❑ Sort a hamper of dirty clothes into lights, darks, and delicates.

❑ Put away anything that is sitting on the washer or dryer that shouldn't be there.

❑ Turn dirty jeans and printed T-shirts inside out and everything else right-side out.

❑ Rinse out and dry any laundry measuring cups/scoops.

5 MINUTES

❑ Vacuum around and behind the washer and dryer to get rid of spiders looking for a warm home and lint that has escaped from the dryer.

❑ Dust shelving that holds supplies and the table or other surface where laundry is folded.

❏ Start a load of laundry or move a load of laundry from the washing machine to the dryer.

❏ Look up your washing machine's model type on the manufacturer's website to find out its maximum limits. After doing this, weigh a load of clothes on your bathroom scale so you can better approximate what a full load of laundry is for your specific washer. (To weigh your clothes: Weigh an empty hamper first, fill it with clothes, weigh it again, and subtract the weight of the hamper to determine the weight of the clothes.) Knowing the limit for your washing machine will ensure you're using it efficiently and effectively for each load.

❏ Hang/lay flat delicate items that can't go into the dryer, or collect any delicate items that have dried, fold them, and put them away.

15 MINUTES

❏ Create a depository for unmatched socks—a decorative "clothes line," a small basket, a large mason jar. Recycle cotton and wool socks that hang out for three months into cleaning rags and toss the ones with man-made fibers.

❏ If you don't like the appearance of the containers for your detergent and other laundry supplies, transfer the supplies to more visually appealing (and well-labeled) containers.

❏ Draft a laundry routine to help you stay current with your laundry. In our family of four, I wash clothes on Mondays, towels and washcloths on Tuesdays, clothes again on Thursdays, and sheets on Fridays. Or, make Monday your son's night, Tuesday your daughter's night, Wednesday your night, and Thursday your spouse's night, to make putting away the clothes easier. Consider putting the load into the wash immediately after getting home from work, moving it to the dryer before dinner, and folding and putting it away after dinner. If you do not have a washer and dryer in your residence, consider going to the laundromat on a set night each week (like Thursdays). Try to pick the night your local laundromat is the least busy so you can use as many machines as necessary. A set weekday routine will also keep you from having to spend your weekends doing laundry.

❏ Fold a load of laundry or put away a load of laundry.

❏ Look around the room—is there anything not laundry-related in this space that is making laundry difficult to do? If so, find a new home for it.

Ten Tips to Make Laundry Easier

1. **DON'T FOLD UNDERWEAR.** It usually doesn't matter if your underwear is wrinkled, so put it in the drawer without folding it. If you have an underwear organizer in your drawer, just stuff a pair of your underwear into each pocket.

2. **BUY ONE TYPE OF CASUAL SOCKS.** Get a pack of a dozen sports socks all the same style, and stop matching and folding socks when you put them in the drawer. When they start to get raggedy, toss them all at the same time in a sock purge and replace with another pack of socks.

3. **BUY IRON-FREE SHIRTS AND SLACKS.** Hang them up as you pull them out of your washer and never iron a shirt or pair of khakis again.

4. **HAVE TOOLS WHERE YOU NEED THEM.** Have a clothing rod, hangers, air-dry rack, waist-high folding table, clean hampers to hold folded clothes, a box or bin for clothes you wish to donate to charity, an iron (for those table linens that rarely come in non-iron fabrics), and a clothes steamer in your laundry room so clothes can be ready to wear when they leave the laundry room and reach your closet.

5. **OWN FEWER CLOTHES.** You can't have Mt. Laundry if your wardrobe isn't large enough to create a mountain of dirty clothes. Also, when you own fewer clothes, it usually means that you have room to store all your clothes. If you don't have room to store all your clothes, you're more likely to have stuff lounging in hampers because you can't put it away.

6. **WEAR FEWER CLOTHES.** As long as they are relatively clean, you don't have to wash your jeans every time you wear them. Outerwear, like sweatshirts and suit jackets, can be worn a few times before needing to be washed. Except for undershirts, T-shirts, underwear, and socks, you may be able to wear a piece of clothing two or three times before it needs to be cleaned. Plan your weekly wardrobe in such a way as to minimize the amount of clothing you dirty.

7. **USE SMALLER HAMPERS.** You're more willing to skip doing the laundry if your hamper isn't full. A smaller hamper will get full more quickly, so you're less likely to skip this chore.

8. **BE INSPIRED.** If you're looking for ideas on how to make your laundry areas more welcoming, head to Pinterest and search for "laundry." You'll be surprised by what a little attention and elbow grease can do for these otherwise dreary spaces.

9. **MAKE LAUNDRY FUN.** (Well, as fun as it can possibly be.) Play music while everyone puts away their clean clothes. Put in a load of wash and then go for a walk or exercise in your favorite way for the duration of the cycle. Put clothes away during the commercial breaks of your favorite television show.

10. **CREATE A LAUNDRY SUPPLY KIT.** If you don't have a washer and/or dryer in your place, make it even easier to cart your supplies back and forth to the laundromat. Pack all your supplies into an easy-to-carry case, like a shower caddy or a house-cleaning supply caddy.

Laundry Bankruptcy

Life happens—your child gets sick when you have a big project due at work; your parents come to visit and your chore schedule is disrupted; an ice storm knocks out your electricity for more than a week—and laundry tends to be the first chore to take a backseat. Once normalcy is established and you're staring at an overwhelming amount of laundry—Mt. Laundry—I vote for you to declare laundry bankruptcy and reset the whole mess in a few hours.

The basic premise of laundry bankruptcy is that instead of spending a week trying to get all of it done at home, you instead take all your dirty clothes to a laundromat.

Once you're at the laundromat, you have a couple of options. If your laundromat offers wash-dry-fold laundering services, you can drop it all off, pay a fee, and come back later to pick it up when it's finished. Fees are usually determined by weight (such as a dollar a pound for permanent press items) with a minimum number of pounds (like ten or fifteen). If you have fifty pounds of clothes, you might end up paying sixty-five or seventy dollars once you include tax and tip. But, this expense might be worth it to you.

Otherwise, if you're like me and don't mind a couple of hours to sit and read a good book, you can take over multiple machines and wash, dry, and fold your clothes yourself at the laundromat. It will still cost you some money (more like fifteen or twenty dollars), but it will save you days of doing this chore at home.

FIVE STEPS TO LAUNDRY BANKRUPTCY

1. Call the laundromat before you head out to make sure it's a slow time there. If the laundromat is packed, you'll waste time going there and coming home without having done your laundry.

2. Take at least twenty dollars in dollar bills and quarters with you. Change machines in laundromats are notorious for being out of order and most machines will only accept coins or singles. On the off chance the washers and dryers require you to use a laundromat-specific debit card, you can always use singles and quarters to put money on it.

3. Take containers of detergent, fabric softener, and whatever supplies you use at home with you to the laundromat.

4. Take a bag, box, or basket with you to use for items you decide to donate to charity. On the way home you can swing by your favorite local charity and make a clothing donation. If it's late in the evening, your donations will at least be ready to be donated during the next drop-off period.

5. Take clean trash bags or enough reusable bags with you to contain your folded laundry when it's ready to go home.

Storing Tools and Hardware

Living requires tools. The most obvious tools are those you rely upon regularly—brooms and screwdrivers and rags and garbage bags. The not-so-obvious tools you require to keep up your home vary depending upon your home's size and whether you own or rent. How you store these utilitarian objects should be the same, however, as they need to be convenient to access, clean, in proper working order, and safely organized to prevent accidents.

When working in this area, ask yourself: *What in this room do I really need and can I not live without? What in this room am I hoarding and have never used and may never have reason to use, while someone else might? Are the items I need in good working order and easy to access when I need them? Are items stored safely so there is very little risk of injury to anyone entering this space?*

30 SECONDS

❏   See a wayward tool? Put it where it belongs.

❏   Pull dust bunnies (or what I refer to as "flugh") from the bottom of brooms, throw away, and wash your hands.

❏   Pull flugh from the brushes of your vacuum cleaner, throw away, and wash your hands.

❏ Turn cleaning supplies so labels face forward for easier identification.

❏ Put dirty rags, sponges, and other items that can be washed into the washing machine for their own trip through the laundry. Sponges and other cleaning materials will likely need to air-dry.

1 MINUTE

❏ Check supplies—paper towels, rags, cleaning liquids, etc.—to see if anything you regularly use needs to be added to your grocery shopping list.

❏ Wipe up any spills or leaks and then put a placemat or shelf liner under liquid bottles to make cleaning easier in the future.

❏ Inspect rubber edges on squeegees, mops, and other items to be sure they're not cracked or damaged. Replace if necessary.

❏ Label spray bottles by writing the contents directly onto the plastic bottle with a black permanent marker. You don't want to accidentally confuse water with ammonia or another chemical.

❏ Inspect the heads of sponge mops, dust mops, and Swiffers to see if any need to be replaced. If so, make a note on your grocery shopping list and include the brand and type of mop. To make it even easier, take a picture of the mop head with your smartphone and then reference the image to ensure you purchase the correct replacement head at the store.

5 MINUTES

❏ Empty your vacuum's canister or replace a full bag.

❏ Gather together cleaning supplies you use regularly and put them into a caddy for ease of transport and use. Consider two or three caddies: one for cleaning supplies for general use around the house, one for bathroom cleaning supplies, and possibly a third for kitchen cleaning supplies. Label each caddy.

❏ Test batteries in flashlights and other battery-charged devices. Replace batteries if necessary.

❏ Bundle extension cords and use Velcro ties or other methods for keeping the cords from becoming tangled. If you're good with knots, search "braid an electrical cord for storing" online for instructional videos. Using a permanent marker, write the length of the cord on one of the plugs for easy reference.

❏ Sort bulk items so all paper towels are together, all toilet paper is together, all tissue boxes are together, all trash bags are together, etc.

15 MINUTES

❏ Inspect tools—screwdrivers, hammers, drills, etc.—for signs of rust or wear. If you detect damage, take them to a local hardware store for repairs. Some hardware stores will also sharpen and provide maintenance services for your tools.

❏ Hang a broom and mop holder on the wall of your utility space to keep these long-handled tools from falling over and off the floor for drying. Label the holder so you know which tool should hang in which holder (and you'll immediately know if one of the items wasn't put away after use). Consider a second holder for short-handled tools like dustpans and hand brooms.

❏ Consider hanging a peg board on an empty wall in this space. Using brackets and other types of hangers made especially for peg boards, hang your most-often-used tools—hammer, level, Phillips screwdriver. Trace around the tools with a permanent marker or label each bracket so it's obvious where to return tools for storage.

❏ Sort small supplies—nails, screws, picture hangers, thumbtacks—into a carrying case that has small compartments. Label each compartment so it's clear what items go in each section. If you have a tool box, be sure that your carrying case fits inside this larger container or buy a tool box that has small compartments in it to store these items.

❏ Vacuum dusters to rid them of dust. If instructions for dusters suggest a different method of cleaning, do what is recommended by the manufacturer. Clean stiff bristles on brushes with a gentle cleanser. Soak and clean any dirty paintbrushes. Write on the handles of any brushes that have a specific purpose—oil paints, varnishes, tile floors, outdoor use only, etc.

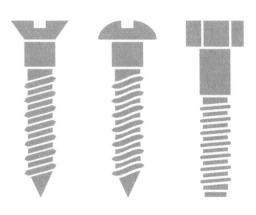

What to Buy in Bulk

Simple-living enthusiasts tend to stay away from buying items in bulk or stashing large quantities of things. There are advantages, however, to buying larger quantities of supplies—prices are usually lower when you buy a package of goods instead of a single item, and you save time by having to go to the store less often. If you have some storage space available, consider having multiples of the following supplies. Before you head to the store, set storage limits (a specific amount of shelf space or a concrete number of objects or one bin to hold all of that one supply) and never go beyond that amount of storage space, regardless of how good the deal is.

- Paper towels

- Toilet paper

- Tissues

- Trash bags of various sizes

- Batteries (mostly rechargeable but some regular for items like smoke detectors)

- Lightbulbs

- Nonperishable dry goods you will consume before they expire

- White vinegar (for cleaning and cooking)

- Sponges

- Powder-free plastic or nitrile gloves to use when cooking and cleaning (latex-free, because houseguests may have latex allergies and latex can interact with some cleaning chemicals)

- Cotton and microfiber rags for cleaning

- Hygiene items you have brand loyalty to (soap, body wash, deodorant)

- Furnace filters

- Liquids (hand soap, laundry detergent) that you decant into smaller containers

- Stamps

- Printer paper

- Blank notecards

It also makes sense to keep supplies (bottled water, ready-to-eat meals, sand, and blankets in your car) on hand in case of an emergency. Learn what natural disasters are common in the part of the country where you live and suggested supplies to store. Also consider items that might be helpful in case of non-natural emergencies, like extended blackouts.

Hallways and Stairs

Admittedly, in the entire existence of the English language, the phrase "What a remarkably well-organized hallway" has likely never been spoken. Although they are often ignored and underappreciated, the passages between rooms in your home shouldn't be havens for clutter or disorder. If you give these areas a little attention, maybe, possibly, someday, someone will comment that they wish they spent more time along these paths in your wonderful home.

When working in this area, ask yourself: *Are the floors completely clear and safe for everyone to pass, including people who may have difficulty walking? Are stair railings helpful instead of a potential hazard? Although halls are tempting places to set additional pieces of narrow furniture (a console table, a bookcase), is the hall realistically wide enough to do so?*

30 SECONDS

❑ Measure the width of a hallway and check to see if there is at least 36 inches of clear space at all points along the passage.

❑ Put away any item on the floor or on a stair, and repeat this action in thirty-second increments until all items are removed from the hallway or staircase.

❑ Wipe down handrails with an appropriate cleaner (dust rag for wood, disinfecting wipe on man-made materials).

❑ Wipe down the doorknob to the main entry door or to rooms along hallways with a disinfecting wipe.

❏ Test doorknobs to make sure they aren't loose. Schedule a time on your calendar to tighten/fix any loose or broken doorknobs.

1 MINUTE

❏ Straighten crooked artwork on walls.

❏ Clean the peephole on the front door's interior or dust/clean the plate of an interior mailbox slot.

❏ Inspect the hallways, staircase, and foyer walls for scuffs, scratches, and dents. If the walls are damaged or dirty, schedule a time on your calendar to repair and/or clean them.

❏ Review all knickknacks and other types of decorative items in your home's hallways and decide if any should be purged. Make a to-do list to get rid of anything you no longer love or you feel no longer represents your design style or has significant signs of deterioration or damage (that you do not wish to repair or maintain).

❏ Label any keys that may belong to doors along the hallway and put these keys in a safe place that is easily accessible in emergencies. If any doorknob has a push-button privacy lock and requires only an unwound paperclip to open, store a few spare paperclips in the same safe place as the keys to ensure you always have one on hand.

5 MINUTES

❏ Tighten screws along handrails, if applicable.

❏ Dust the spindles and banister on a staircase railing.

❏ Vacuum hall runners, interior throw rugs near the main entrance, and hallway carpeting.

❏ Sweep the foyer and hallways with wood, tile, or laminate flooring.

❏ Empty the contents of a console table drawer. Purge any clutter and find new storage locations for anything that is not appropriate for this drawer. To help organize the contents of the drawer, set a drawer organizer in the drawer before returning the items that belong in this space. If you don't have a manufactured drawer organizer, see page 103 for advice on how to create your own.

15 MINUTES

❏ If you need to move any piece of furniture out of a hallway so that the hallway has 36 inches of cleared space, take fifteen minutes and relocate the furniture (or boxes or whatever was blocking the passage).

❏ Using the hose attachment of your vacuum, start at the bottom of the stairs and vacuum up the staircase.

❏ Repair any squeaky stair(s) per DIY instructions relevant to your type of staircase. A screw might need to be tightened where the stair connects to a riser. Or if a stair is cracked or in need of significant repair beyond your level of expertise, contact a specialist (such as a carpenter) and schedule an appointment to have the stair repaired/replaced.

❏ Evaluate the lighting in your hallways, staircases, and foyer. Are all the bulbs in working order? Replace any burned-out bulbs. Do chandeliers emit enough overhead light to keep these areas safe? Does any art-work need picture or display lighting? If any lights or chandeliers need to be changed/installed, set up an appointment with an electrician to make these changes.

❏ Tighten all the loose doorknobs in your home. If they have a metal finish that requires polishing, do that, too. Polishing gloves are easiest to use for polishing doorknobs.

The Table of No Return

My friends Alice and Brad have a console table near the entrance to their condo that they have aptly named the Table of No Return. Like the Hotel California in the Eagles song of the same name, their stuff is set on the table but it feels like it "can never leave." You may have a similar table in your home, or maybe your no-return location is a kitchen counter or dining room buffet, where stuff unfortunately goes to reside almost permanently. If there is a location like this in your home, this weekend project is your chance to clear off this cluttered surface once and for all.

WHAT YOU'LL NEED: A laundry hamper, a trash bag, a recycling bin, a pen or pencil, a notepad, and appropriate decorative items for the table/surface.

NO MORE NO RETURN!

After acquiring the necessary supplies, mentally divide your table into sections—based on the size of your cluttered surface, you may decide to visualize four, six, or eight work areas. If you're a literal thinker, you might even choose to lay string or dental floss on the surface to provide actual lines.

Once your lines are established, your plan will be to unclutter a section, put away all the items in your laundry hamper from that section, and then take a ten- or fifteen-minute break before returning to work on the next section and repeating the process. After uncluttering, you'll establish habits to put an end to your Table of No Return permanently.

When uncluttering a section, immediately trash or recycle any items you wish to purge (these might be old receipts for items you have already consumed, junk mail, etc.). Any item you wish to keep, write it down in your notebook (paperwork, library book, winter coats, tax forms, hemming project, pocket change, etc.) and then place the item in your laundry hamper.

When the section is sorted fully into purge and keep groups, you'll need to find permanent storage homes for everything you have decided to keep. Work your way through your laundry hamper, putting everything away. When this step is complete, take a ten- or fifteen-minute break before starting again with the next section. Repeat this process until the surface is uncluttered and then take out the trash bag and recycling so they don't clutter up your home.

Once all the clutter has been removed from your table/surface, you need to address the actual problem of this area being a clutter deposit site. The next thing you need to do is create a diversion that makes it difficult to use the surface as a clutter magnet. If your surface is a console table, you may wish to decorate it with a table runner and a flower arrangement or sculpture. A tablecloth, centerpiece, and placemats can be set upon a dining table to make it less inviting for clutter. A kitchen counter can have a temporary sign taped to it reminding people not to set anything in that spot to discourage clutter buildup and encourage new, more organized habits.

After creating decorative diversions, reflect upon the notes you took about the types of items that regularly cluttered up your table/space. Your goal at this point is to find more convenient spaces and efficient processes for these items moving forward, because your current storage location and habit isn't working. This may mean you need to create a drop zone (see page 18 for instructions) if mail, paperwork, coats, pet leashes, and bags are part of your clutter issue.

If library books or textbooks are a common issue for you, a decorative bin or side table might be necessary near the main entrance to your home to hold them. You may want to hang a magazine rack on your wall to catch the day's newspaper or magazines you're reading.

Know yourself and your roommates'/family's current habits to help you creatively generate new storage solutions and habits. Try a solution for two or three weeks and then make any necessary adjustments to continue to keep clutter off your former Table of No Return.

Garage and Automobiles

In addition to storing your car, the room with a movable wall is often a catchall storage space for anything that isn't temperature-sensitive. It can become such a catchall that it stops being a place to house your car and transforms into a clutter storage unit. If you'd like a place that doesn't make your blood boil and protects your car during the next hailstorm, clearing clutter from your garage can bring you a sense of calm and your automobile some protection.

When working in this area, ask yourself: *Is everything in this area stored safely? Are chemicals, tools, and pieces of equipment stored in such a way as to be easily retrieved when needed? Can I park a car in the garage? Can people get in and out of the car easily and without damaging the vehicle? Is there anything in the garage that should be stored in a more climate-controlled area of my home?*

NOTE: If you store many home utility items (brooms, extension cords, small tools) in your garage, be sure to check out Storing Tools and Hardware on page 147 for even more ideas.

30 SECONDS

❏ Scan your car for trash, and throw away or recycle anything that doesn't belong.

❏ See something out of place or on its side? Put it where it belongs or set it upright.

❏ Turn all cleaning supplies, dry goods, and similar products so the labels face forward for easier identification.

❏ Check all lights inside and adjacent to the garage to make sure they are in working order.

❏ Label automatic garage door openers to indicate which bay (if you have a multicar garage) they belong to and/or in which car the opener typically resides.

1 MINUTE

❏ Gather up like items (such as golf equipment or bicycling accessories) and store them together on a shelf or in a bin or other storage container.

❏ Check to make sure storage containers are properly closed to deter pests, spills, and other messes.

❏ Clean doorknobs, doorbells, automatic garage door opener buttons on walls, or garage door handles with a disinfecting wipe.

❏ Open garage door(s) and quickly brush leaves from the lip of the door(s) using a stiff broom or a dry rag.

❏ Lie on your stomach and inspect the floor for small nails or other objects that have the potential to cause trouble for car/bike tires. If you find any objects, return them to their proper storage locations or throw them away to prevent future accidents.

5 MINUTES

❏ Dust shelves and surfaces.

❏ Clean the windows of your car or of the garage door.

❏ Sweep the floor of the garage and areas immediately in front of the bay(s) outside the garage door(s).

❏ Pour kitty litter onto floor stains made by oil or other fluids, stomp the litter in with your feet, wait a few hours, and then sweep up the litter. (Actual work time is brief.)

❏ Label the exterior (using a permanent marker or printed sticker) of all storage containers indicating what is inside the container. Keep the categories broad, but helpful: holiday decorations, lacrosse gear, lawn mower maintenance tools. You may find it most convenient to label both the top and the sides of the container.

15 MINUTES

❏ Vacuum the seats and floors of your car.

❏ Install a garage floor covering where your car is typically parked to protect your floor from oil and other automobile fluid leaks.

❏ Hose off mud, dirt, and grime from any outdoor children's toys, basketball hoops, soccer nets, bicycles, scooters, and other larger pieces of sporting equipment.

❑ Clean any mildew off the walls near the garage door or an exterior door with a mixture of a hefty squeeze of liquid dishwashing detergent in a half-filled bucket of warm water. Use a soft rag to scrub the wall with the cleaning mixture and a dry, clean rag to remove any excess water after cleaning. If the drywall or concrete block is damaged in any way beneath the mildew, contact a home repair specialist to schedule an appointment to have the damage repaired. Crumbling drywall makes it extremely simple for pests to enter your home, so make the appointment earlier rather than later.

❑ At the bare minimum, take your car to the car wash at the end of every season and to be detailed once a year. This is likely to take more than fifteen minutes, but your time commitment only involves driving to the car wash or detail shop and then home again. You can read or answer e-mails or do other work while you wait for your car. Call ahead to learn when the car wash or detail shop is least busy during the week, then go during that window (or make an appointment) so it will take the least amount of time possible. Chemicals and dirt get ground into your paint job and dirt breaks down carpet and upholstery fibers, so regular cleaning helps extend the life and quality of your car.

A Gratifying Garage

Every few years, your garage likely demands a little extra attention. Things are set somewhere in a hurry and forgotten, or your interests have changed but retired sports equipment still lingers. Whatever the cause, making over your garage is a wonderful activity for clear skies and 70°F weather.

Each garage is different, and what is stored in it varies widely from household to household. As you work through this project, attune yourself to your specific needs and adjust the advice accordingly.

WHAT YOU'LL NEED: Lawn and garden trash bags; a recycling bin; work gloves; a large tarp; a broom and dustpan (and possibly a shop vacuum); a bucket with a cleaning solution (a hefty squeeze of liquid dishwashing detergent in a half-full bucket of water); multiple dry, clean cotton rags; a box of kitty litter (if you have stains on the floor of your garage); tools (hammer, screwdrivers, etc.); a garage floor covering (if you don't already have it under your vehicles); a shelving system (if you don't already have one); and storage containers.

CREATE A GRATIFYING GARAGE!

The first steps in your garage makeover project are relatively simple but will likely take a good amount of time, so I recommend getting started early in the day. After gathering your necessary supplies, lay a tarp in your yard and/or driveway and move everything that isn't attached to the walls, floor, or ceiling out of your garage and onto the tarp. Any obvious trash or recycling you come across during this process can immediately be disposed of. While you work, also pay attention to the types of things you currently keep in your garage.

Once everything is out of the garage, it's time to give the space a solid cleaning—dust, scrub, sweep/shop vac, and polish. Wear your work gloves for this part of the process and get rid of those spiderwebs and floor stains. As you work, if you notice anything that needs to be repaired, either take care of it yourself right then or schedule time for a professional to address the issue. (If you need to call in a professional, continue to work today but avoid the area that will have to be repaired and temporarily store items for that area in another location.)

Now that your space is clean, it's time to address your shelving and storage options. Many companies have relatively easy-to-install garage storage systems. Look for material that won't easily rust and is manufactured to store lots of weight for an extended period of time—avoid wood because it warps and easily acquires mold and mildew.

DIY TIP:
CREATE YOUR OWN STORAGE SYSTEM

Umbrella stands are great for holding lacrosse and hockey sticks or baseball bats. A clothes hamper can corral soccer balls, footballs, baseballs, and basketballs. When it comes to storage bins and boxes, steer clear of natural materials like cardboard or paper, wood, and woven-fiber baskets, which are tasty treats for pests. Clear plastic bins are great because you can see their contents and they deter mold and mildew.

Your next step is to sort through everything outside on the tarp. Do the following actions outside—avoid the temptation to begin putting things away at this point. As with so many uncluttering and organizing projects, you'll want to begin this stage by sorting like items with like items (all hammers together, all tennis rackets together, all bikes, etc.). You'll also want to put any trash you find into a trash bag, recycling into the recycling bin, items you wish to sell or give away in their own pile, and any items that belong inside your house instead of in the garage in a separate pile. If there is anything that needs to be repaired, you can write it down on a list.

Next, examine all of your piles of similar things. Do you have unnecessary duplicates of items? Items you have replaced without purging the original? Items damaged beyond repair? Open all storage boxes/containers and examine the contents. In addition to deciding what to keep and what to purge from each of the containers, determine whether that storage container is the best place for each object. Continue to trash the trash you find, recycle the recycling, pull out items you don't want and move them into a sell or give-away pile, and move anything that is in the wrong place to a more appropriate pile.

When you have finished uncluttering, it's time to return items to the garage in an organized manner. Like items should continue to be stored together: All tools should be in the same area (like a workbench or section of shelving) and specific types of tools should be kept together in that area (hammers with hammers and screwdrivers with screwdrivers). Small items, like screws and nails, should be stored in divided containers so they remain separated and don't get lost. Heavy items should be stored on the bottom of shelving to help stabilize the storage system, and the items you access most often should be in the most convenient location to access (for most people this is waist height). Only very light items, like containers storing packing peanuts, should be above shoulder height. Label containers by writing the contents on the box/bin/bucket/jar with permanent marker or by printing adhesive labels and sticking them to the containers.

As you work through your garage makeover, take breaks as necessary, drink plenty of water, and remember that sometimes things look bad before they get better.

Guest Bedroom

In homes that have separate rooms or parts of rooms for guests, it can be easy to forget that the sofa that has become a dumping ground for magazines is really a pull-out bed where your mother-in-law plans to sleep the next time she's in town. It's wise to utilize these rooms for multiple purposes, but it's important to establish boundaries so you're always ready to be a good host.

When working in this area, ask yourself: *Is this space welcoming and ready to be used by guests? If this room also doubles (or even triples) its purpose as something like a home office or a hobby workspace, is there a way for these tasks to be accomplished in other areas of the home when I have visitors?*

30 SECONDS

❏ Move as many items off the guest bed as you can and return them to their appropriate storage places.

❏ Check "Guest Retreat" supplies (see page 175) to see if anything needs to be repaired, replaced, or restocked.

❏ Clear wayward items that have accumulated on top of a nightstand and any seating beyond the bed.

❏ Check the alarm clock in this room and make sure it displays the correct time as well as has battery backup in case the electricity goes out.

❏ Check the nightlight in the bedroom to see if it continues to illuminate. Replace it if necessary with a long-lasting LED nightlight.

1 MINUTE

❏ Empty the wastebasket and return it to a place easily reached by someone lying in the bed.

❏ If the room serves multiple purposes, create a physical boundary (such as a strip of masking tape on the carpet) to delineate where the guest room ends and the craft room/home office/home gym begins. Moving forward, respect these boundaries and don't allow items from one space to cross into other territories. Remove the physical boundary before guests arrive.

❏ Cover the bed after it's made up (comforter, spare blanket, pillows, etc.) with a large flat sheet to protect against dust and pet hair. Remove the flat sheet before guests arrive.

❏ Remove any outdated reading materials.

❏ Inspect any guest comfort items—such as a bedside carafe and cup or a spare pair of slippers—for damage and wear and replace if necessary.

5 MINUTES

❏ Clear space in a dresser drawer and closet so visitors will have a place to put their things when staying in this room.

❏ Think like a houseguest and determine what might make visitors feel unwelcome or like they are intruding in this space. If a room serves double duty (like home office and guest room) remove things like papers or items that are infringing on the bed. Create a list of to-do actions to rectify these items.

❏ Place a drawer organizer with dividers into a nightstand drawer. Place guest items stored in the nightstand (see page 175) into divisions of the drawer organizer, being sure to leave an open space for eyeglasses. Lie on the bed while doing this to ensure all items in the drawer are easy to retrieve from a prone position.

❏ Clean the interiors of the windows and vacuum the windowsill, especially in anticipation of guests if you have a spectacular view from the window or don't have central air or a ceiling fan in the room.

❏ Vacuum the headboard, under the nightstand, and any seating and under that seating, and do a quick pass along the curtains (using an upholstery attachment on your vacuum hose) in anticipation of guests.

15 MINUTES

❏ If this is a multipurpose space, such as a guest room and home office, brainstorm ways to conceal the other purpose(s) of the room from guests. Would installing a screen or divider be helpful? Can you put files in drawers instead of boxes?

❏ Pull out everything that is stored under the bed. Clean under the bed (vacuum and/or dust mop) and wipe down the legs and supports for the bed with a clean rag. As you work, remember your guests might be snoopy, so try not to store anything under the guest bed that you wouldn't want your mother to discover.

❑ At least twice a year, launder the comforter/duvet cover and duvet, spare blanket, decorative pillow covers, and pillows.

❑ If the doorknob to this room doesn't have a push-button privacy lock (not a keyed lock, but one that can be opened from the hallway with a paperclip in an emergency), strongly consider replacing it with a door-knob that does. This is especially important if you use the room for other purposes and you or your children may momentarily forget you have guests and accidentally walk in on them.

❑ It will obviously take more than fifteen minutes, but spend a night sleeping on your guest bed. Identify any areas of discomfort you felt during the night. Can you add a mattress pad with a pillow top to the bed? Do you need to oil the bedsprings to reduce squeaks? If the bed is a pull-out couch or other type of transformative furniture, are all the moving parts working correctly and in good condition? If you find any change you wish to make, schedule time on your calendar to address these issues.

Create a Guest Retreat

A well-organized guest room has many benefits: your guests feel truly welcome, they are able to address many issues on their own instead of asking you for every detail and amenity about their stay, and once the room is uncluttered, cleaned, and organized (see page 171), you're ready for guests regardless of how much notice you receive in advance of their visit.

When creating a guest room (or, in my family's case, a pull-out couch in the living room), try to make the space as much as you can like a lavish hotel that doesn't skimp on the details. What amenities might you wish to provide to your guests?

NOTES: If you don't have a room with a door for your guests, consider storing these items in a lidded box that is large enough to hold them all. You can quickly pull the box out of a closet before your guests arrive and set up the space. Then, after your guests leave, simply wash the linens and restock the bin so it's ready the next time overnight guests appear at your door.

If you have a guest room, you should still consider storing many of your supplies in a lidded box. However, your storage container won't need to be as large as it will for individuals without a dedicated room, because items like the duvet, duvet cover, mattress cover, pillows, blanket, and one set of sheets will be on the bed and some items can be left out as decoration, like the alarm clock.

CREATE A GUEST RETREAT!

Assemble a folder containing the following information:

- A welcome letter for your future guests
- Your home's physical address, including unit number if applicable
- Your mailing address (if different from your physical address)
- Your home's phone number

- Cell phone numbers for everyone who resides at your home
- Company names and office numbers for everyone who resides at your home
- Your home's Wi-Fi network name and current password
- Local emergency numbers and address of closest hospital and police station
- Address and/or directions to closest gas station, noting if the station has diesel
- Address and/or directions to preferred grocery store
- Address and/or directions to preferred national-chain pharmacy
- Address and/or directions to favorite area coffee shop
- Addresses, names, and types of cuisine for many local restaurants. Consider also listing your favorite dish or the signature entrée offered by the restaurant.
- Addresses of any must-see attractions within walking distance of your home
- A list of local parks for kids and trails for running or taking walks
- Address of the closest laundromat or directions on how to operate your home's washer and dryer and location of necessary supplies
- Instructions for how to set the current time and the alarm on the provided alarm clock

Items for the bed:

- Nice sheets and pillowcases—high-thread-count cotton for warm months and soft fleece or flannel sheets for cold months
- Two pillows, one firm and one less so, with a synthetic filling (some guests may have allergies to down)
- Two zip-close pillow covers to protect pillows
- Appropriate-size mattress cover. If children will stay in your guest space, consider a waterproof mattress cover. I recommend the Luna Premium Hypoallergenic Waterproof Mattress Protector because it doesn't feel like plastic or crinkle.
- Pillow topper for mattress if, as in our home, the mattress on the pull-out couch is decent, but far from lavish

- Hypoallergenic duvet in a medium weight and soft duvet cover
- Coordinating medium-weight blanket

Additional items:

- A spare house key
- A guidebook to local attractions and, if applicable, a guidebook for the public transit system (like the subway or metro). Feel welcome to add your own notes to these books, especially favorite stops and why.
- Two sets of towels and washcloths
- Carafe and water glass
- Doily, coaster, or trivet to place under carafe if nightstand is made of wood
- Wind-up alarm clock, so you don't have to worry about replacing batteries or locating an electrical plug
- Box of tissues
- Small container of quality hand lotion
- Small container of aspirin, acetaminophen, and/or ibuprofen
- LED flashlight
- LED nightlight
- Small notepad and pen
- Collapsible laundry hamper

Pet Places

Sharing a home with a pet comes with a good amount of stuff, even with low-key pets like fish. Keeping all your pet items uncluttered ensures that your pet stays healthy, safe, and happy.

When working in this area, ask yourself: *Am I caring for my pet's items with the same care I'm giving to items of mine? Are any of my pet's items in disrepair and needing to be replaced? Are there items I'm not using that a local shelter or vet might benefit from having instead (old sheets and towels, for example)?*

30 SECONDS

- ❏ Round up any wayward pet items (food, toy, brush) and return the items to their proper storage spot.

- ❏ Remove pet hair from a pet comb or brush and dispose of it.

- ❏ Close closet doors to keep furry friends from leaving pet hair on clean clothes and other stored items.

- ❏ Pick up any small items you see on the floor that your pet might accidentally ingest (strings, pieces of paper, small bits of chocolate, onions, grapes, rubber bands, pennies, and other choking hazards).

- ❏ Unplug your shredder or enable its child safety lock so your pet won't accidentally activate the shredding mechanism.

1 MINUTE

❏ Wipe or buff the exterior of your aquarium with the manufacturer's recommended cleanser.

❏ Close the lid on any open trash can in your home if you have a cat or a dog. If your trash cans do not have lids, consider replacing them if digging through the trash is something your pet could do (even if she hasn't shown interest in the past).

❏ Close the lid on any open toilet in your home if you have a cat or a dog.

❏ If you have furry pets, replace your vacuum's filter with the manufacturer's recommended HEPA filter, which will be more effective at catching dust mites and pet dander than a regular filter.

❏ Untangle dog leashes and hang them near the main entrance to your home.

5 MINUTES

❏ Clean a litter box or your pet's equivalent.

❏ Vacuum living room furniture to remove pet hair or use a dust mop under furniture to remove any hair that may be trapped underneath.

❏ Clean a cat/dog door with a damp cloth to remove hair, dirt, and grime.

❏ Wash pet toys in the washing machine or dishwasher, based on the manufacturer's recommendations.

❏ If you have a furry pet, give him/her a thorough brushing to reduce the amount of fur and pet dander that might otherwise be deposited around your home. I strongly recommend the FURminator for dogs and cats, as it is well made and will last for the life of your pet.

15 MINUTES

❏ Type up and print instructions for how to care for your pet when you travel. Save this file to your computer's hard drive so all you have to do is print it for your pet sitter the next time you leave town.

❏ Clean the interior of your rodent, amphibian, small mammal, bird, or reptile aquarium or cage.

❏ Acquire baskets or bins for your pet's items. For example, if you have a dog, you'll likely want a small storage container for toys that you will keep in the living room. Pet hair care and/or skin care items should be in a container near where you groom your pet. Dry and moist pet food should be stored in an airtight container to retain its freshness. Litter and wood chips should be contained to reduce mess. In your utility closet where cleaning supplies are stored, be sure to have an area or bin especially for cleaners that help remove pet stains. Except for a basket holding toys, be sure to label all other pet-related containers so their contents are easy for pet sitters to locate and identify.

❏ Make a first-aid kit for your pet. Talk with your vet about what to include in the kit and ask for first-aid reference materials to also include. Label the kit and store it in an easily accessible location in your home. If you have a dog that you regularly take on hikes, consider a travel-style pet first-aid kit that you can put in your car's trunk along with your human first-aid kit in case of an emergency while hiking.

❏ Remove, wash, and dry the cover of your cat and/or dog bed(s).

Stuff in Any or Many Rooms

Janine Adams, a professional organizer with Peace of Mind Organizing and OrganizeYourFamilyHistory .com who has appeared on A&E's *Hoarders* and TLC's *Hoarding: Buried Alive*, on the tip she gives most often to clients:

More than anything, I probably hear myself telling people to use labels. When I see failed systems in clients' homes, more often than not it's because they did not label containers or shelves and family members were not able to put things into their new homes. Using labels is like a little insurance policy for new organizing systems.

Books and Entertainment

Books, television, movies, music, and board and video games keep us entertained when we're in the confines of our homes. A well-curated and organized collection also makes enjoying these diversions that much more rewarding. Although they are usually welcome additions to our possessions, books and other forms of entertainment tend to be much more difficult to part with when they transform into clutter. We hold on to them as reminders of times when we laughed or smiled or learned something new about who we are. But clutter is clutter, and getting rid of the old to make room for the new is a very satisfying endeavor.

When working with these items, ask yourself: *Am I keeping any books, movies, CDs, or other forms of entertainment that I never plan to read, watch, or listen to again? Are there books on my shelves for the purpose of impressing visitors instead of enriching my life? Are all of my forms of media organized in a manner that makes retrieving and returning items as simple as possible? What clutter can I remove from this space so I can make room for future acquisitions?*

30 SECONDS

❏ Remove one (or more) book, movie, CD, or video game from your collection that you'll never read, watch, reference, or play again, and set it in a box of items you plan to sell or give away. When the box is full, sell or donate its contents.

❏ Flip through a book you plan to sell or give away and make sure it doesn't contain any personal notes, annotations, or sticky notes. Remove these items if you encounter them.

❏ Recycle the day's newspaper or other periodicals that have been read.

❏ Return to its shelf, drawer, or other storage system any media that is not in its proper storage location.

❏ Clean remote controls and/or game controllers with a disinfecting wipe.

1 MINUTE

❏ Dust the tops and fronts of books on a shelf.

❏ Save/import a music CD to iTunes (or equivalent).

❏ Find a storage space for all your remotes (television, DVD player, DVR, receiver) so that you always return the remotes to the same space after every use.

❏ Store a rare and/or antique book in an appropriate-size archival-quality box made specifically for storing books.

❏ Check out CanIStream.it to learn if a movie you own on DVD is available to watch through a streaming service you already subscribe to (Hulu Plus, Netflix, Amazon Prime, etc.). If it is, strongly consider selling or giving away the DVD.

5 MINUTES

❏ If you have numerous cookbooks, pull out any you haven't used. Schedule time to review the books and then set on your weekly meal plan a time when you can create something from the books. Give yourself three months, and if there are books you still haven't made a single recipe from after that time, donate those books to your local library.

❑ Stand up straight any books on your bookshelves that are leaning by using bookends to hold them in the upright position. Leaning damages a book's spine. Try your best not to store books flat, but if you have to for size considerations, lay the books in a pile where the bottom book is the longest and widest book, moving up in size to the shortest and narrowest book (so your books look like a triangle). Don't stack books more than a foot high, to keep from warping the books at the bottom of the pile.

❑ Similar to books, store DVDs, vinyl records, CDs, etc., in the upright position to reduce chances of warping. The exception to this would be if you store these items in an organizer that provides space between each disc so the weight of each item is directly supported by a divider, not another case or disc.

❑ Return dust jackets to any books not currently being read.

❑ Secure knickknacks (vases, small sculptures) on bookshelves and media centers to the shelf with clear museum gel (such as Ready America brand) that is manufactured to be used with the materials of your shelves and your knickknack.

15 MINUTES

❑ Organize your media in an obvious way that makes retrieving and returning it super easy for you and others—alphabetical by author/editor/publisher/composer/performance/game name, by topic, by Dewey Decimal or Library of Congress classification, etc.

❏ If your media is currently stored in an unfinished basement, attic, or garage or is exposed to direct sunlight, strongly consider moving it. Extreme heat, humidity, and sunlight can damage these items. If you choose to keep books and entertainment, take care of what you choose to keep.

❏ For any media you wish to keep in physical form, consider creating a digital database or simple spreadsheet as an inventory of your media. There is software available to do this (Delicious Library, for example) where you can scan the media's barcode with your smartphone's camera and it loads in the cover image, author name, publication date, actors, composers, etc., and allows you to share with friends.

❏ Sort through all the magazines and newspapers that you store in racks, side tables, or the equivalent in your home. Recycle any newspapers more than two days old. Recycle any magazines more than three months old. Check the periodicals' websites to see if you can locate favorite articles online instead of being tempted to keep them. If you can't find an article online, scan the specific article and save it to your computer.

❏ Invest in a universal remote (such as one of the Logitech Harmony universal remotes) and then program it to work with all your electronics. Also, install the cradle charger in a convenient location to make charging extremely simple.

Digitize Your Bookshelf

When the second-generation Kindle electronic book readers were released, I bought one. Not to be overly dramatic, but it changed my life. I had always been a reader—at least one book a week after my mastery of the English language got me to chapter books. But after I got a Kindle, I went from being someone who read fifty-two books a year to being someone who reads triple or quadruple that. The convenience of getting most any book I want exactly when I want it without having to store it on a shelf . . . swoon!

In addition to improved accessibility and the reduction of clutter, electronic books are fantastic for people like me who have poor eyesight. On almost all brands of e-readers, you can adjust the size of the typeface to make it larger and even increase the amount of space between lines of text. In most cases, the digital version of the book is also less expensive than the print version. And many public libraries have digital lending programs, too. Monthly subscription services like Kindle Unlimited function similarly for books as services like Netflix and Hulu Plus do for movies and TV shows.

If you are able or interested in making the leap to electronic book readers, I'll admit it makes uncluttering your physical books much simpler. You can use these tips for culling your book collection even if you don't have an e-reader, but you may decide to be less cutthroat in your decision-making process.

These are the types of books you may wish to **KEEP:**

- Children's books, especially if you have children
- First editions of antique books that are valuable
- Books that are out of print and impossible to find digitally
- Cookbooks that you regularly use, especially if you do not have a tablet you feel comfortable using in the kitchen
- Reference and resource books (like this one)
- Books signed by the author or inscribed to you from someone you love
- Copies of your own book, if you are an author
- Books that for reasons you cannot explain are part of your soul (if you don't know what I'm talking about, you can move along to the next item)

- Coffee-table books you set out regularly and view
- Personal journals
- How-to books with lots of graphics that may not correlate well to digital formats
- Family Bibles or religious texts that record births, deaths, and other important dates

These are the types of books you may wish to **SELL OR GIVE AWAY:**

- All other books

If you decide you wish to sell your books, I've found the biggest bang for your books comes through being a used-book seller on Amazon. It takes time to do it this way, because you have to mail directly to all the people who buy your books individually. If selling isn't a priority to you, simply contact your local public library and ask if they have a donation program, or donate to your favorite local charity shop.

Papers, Bills, and Subscriptions

Catalogs, junk mail, magazines, bills, and other correspondence flood into your home daily, and it can be difficult to know what to keep and what to purge. And, like a flood, you may have little control over how much comes in. When in possession of the right tools, you can survive the flood and come out swimmingly.

When working with these items, ask yourself: *Do I need to keep and file a physical copy of this paper for legal or tax reasons? If not, do I need to scan it or can I simply shred it straightaway? Does this bill provider have online and/or automatic payment options? Does my bank offer direct payment/deposit or bill-paying services? Am I using/reading/ participating in the subscriptions that come through my door? Can I request that a catalog/magazine/newsletter no longer come to my physical mailbox?*

30 SECONDS

❏ In early November, write "Catalogs" on the side of a box. Then, in the months of November and December, drop all unwanted catalogs you receive into the box. Save the box for the "unsubscribe" project mentioned in the 15-minute section.

❏ Each time you receive a piece of mail you don't want to shred or re-cycle, immediately write on the envelope what the next action is for that piece of paper before putting it in a physical inbox: *File under IRA Statements, Sign by X date, Keep until X date and then dispose, Read by X date,* etc.

❏ Pull papers out of your backpack, briefcase, or purse and put the papers where they should be properly stored (such as in your home office's inbox) until you can process them.

❏ Break down a cardboard box for recycling.

❏ Shred ¼ to ½ inch of documents in your shred pile.

1 MINUTE

❏ Sign on to your bank's website and read their directions for automatic bill-payment services.

❏ Sign on to your bank's website and request digital bank statements and unsubscribe from printed ones. If you're already getting digital statements from your bank, sign on to your credit card and investments' websites, request digital statements, and unsubscribe from printed ones.

❏ As you receive paper bills, sign on to the company's website and see if there are automatic bill-payment services available.

❏ File a handful of papers marked "To Be Filed" from your physical inbox.

❏ Scan and save in the appropriate digital folders a handful of documents marked "To Be Scanned" from your physical inbox.

5 MINUTES

☐ Based on what you learned about automatic bill-payment services, sign up for as many automatic payment options as possible and request that paper copies of your bills are no longer mailed to your home. Be sure to learn how to see and download your monthly statement, too.

☐ Create a file structure on your computer to store digital copies of your bills and banking statements.

☐ Review the papers in a file folder (or more than one folder, if time permits). Remove any papers you no longer wish to keep in that folder and shred or recycle them. Scan anything that can be digitized and be sure to save any papers you need to keep in physical form. For a detailed list of what to keep, scan, and shred, see page 198.

☐ Search online to learn what your state's laws are regarding which documents need to be saved in physical form for the purposes of filing your annual state taxes and for how long you need to retain these documents (such as receipts, stock transfers, anything that you referenced when compiling your tax return for tax deductions or credits). The IRS requires you to keep these support documents for three years in case you are audited at the national level, but some states have a longer timeframe. If you cannot find this retention information online, contact a local accountant. Once every few years, return to your state's website to see if this length of time has changed.

☐ List your magazine subscriptions and then determine if there are any magazines on the list you don't read cover-to-cover. Any that you don't typically read, sign into the magazine's subscription site and cancel an automatic renewal if you have one. If you don't have an automatic renewal, simply make a note on your calendar to not renew the subscription when it expires. If you are unaware of when your subscription is up for renewal, you can sometimes locate this information on the address label. Tablet owners also may wish to consider switching print magazine subscriptions to digital ones through services like Zinio.

15 MINUTES

❏ In January, sign up for CatalogChoice.org (an unsubscribe service) or a similar service. Go through the box of unwanted catalogs and solicitations you gathered in November and December (see project in 30-second section) and report to the service the catalogs you've collected. As the year progresses, report any additional catalogs you receive that you do not want to receive. DMAChoice.org also provides you with the opportunity to be removed from all direct mail advertisements beyond catalogs.

❏ Opt out of all credit card offers by following the suggestion of the Federal Trade Commission (FTC) and call toll-free 1-888-5-OPT-OUT (1-888-567-8688) or visit OptOutPrescreen.com. You have the choice to opt out for five years or permanently.

❏ Label files in your filing cabinet with labels made with a label maker or a printer. The easier the labels are to read, the faster your retrieval time will be.

❏ Order from the appropriate state offices duplicate copies of your most vital documents to store in your fireproof safe in case of an emergency. Documents you may wish to request: birth, marriage, divorce, death, Social Security, and military records. You also may choose to keep a copy of these documents in your filing cabinet for easier access.

❏ If you have competition for services in your area (cable providers, trash collection), research to see if you are paying the lowest price for the quality of service you desire. Companies are eager to retain their clients, so call your current providers' customer service lines to see if they have any deals or strategies for reducing your monthly fees.

SWIMMING IN SUBSCRIPTIONS?

I love magazines, which is likely why I so often work with them. The glossy paper! The insights from people in easy-to-digest lengths and formats! I even get a small rush when I find them in my mailbox. However, I've learned over the years that receiving any more than three a month results in them languishing in my magazine rack, cluttering it up. If you currently have more subscriptions than you are reading each month, follow these steps to see how many subscriptions are actually right for you.

1. When a magazine arrives, write the date of arrival on the cover with a permanent marker.
2. Each time you pick up the magazine to read something in it, write that date on the cover.
3. When you've read it cover-to-cover, put a giant X on the cover.
4. When the next issue of the magazine arrives, do the same thing.

At the end of three months, lay out all your subscriptions on your dining table. Are there any without Xs? Are there any with only a single date—the date the magazine arrived—on the cover? Cancel all the subscriptions that have only one date on them and nothing else. Then, be honest with yourself about all the subscriptions that failed to get a single X on their cover. Those subscriptions might be good contenders for cancellations, too.

Keep It, Scan It, or Shred It?

A common sentiment I hear about papers is: "I don't know what I'm supposed to keep, so I keep pretty much everything." This method is certainly thorough, but it's completely unnecessary—plus it's a poor use of space and time. Make your life easier by learning what to keep, scan, and shred.

NOTE: As a word of caution, if for any reason you have been advised by your accountant or another legal entity to follow different rules, please follow their advice. Also, except for the first list of items, you should scan every document you plan to keep and back up the file to an online storage service. If at any time something were to happen to your home and your important documents were destroyed, you would be very grateful to have a digital copy of these important papers.

PAPERS YOU CAN IMMEDIATELY RECYCLE OR SHRED

- Junk mail
- Old catalogs, magazines, and newspapers you never plan to read again
- Personal correspondence you never plan to read again
- Receipts for consumable goods (like a cup of coffee) you've already consumed and that you paid for with cash. The exceptions to this rule would be if the purchase would need to be used as a proof of purchase for claiming deductions or credits when filing your taxes or if you would like to record the cash purchase for budgeting purposes (after you record it, toss it).

PAPERS YOU CAN SCAN AND THEN SHRED MONTHLY

- Receipts, once you have reconciled them with your monthly bank and credit card statements
- Copies of deposit slips, once you have reconciled them with your monthly bank, credit card, and/or investment statements

PAPERS YOU CAN SCAN AND THEN SHRED ANNUALLY

- Pay stubs, after you have reconciled them with your annual tax statement from your employer(s)
- Monthly bank, credit card, and investment statements, after you have reconciled them with your annual statements. If you are creating a budget, you may wish to keep the monthly statements a little longer until the same month pops back up on the calendar so you can compare your regular expenses for that month for future planning. For example, shred your July 2017 statement after you compare it to your July 2018 statement.
- Similar to the previous item, your monthly Social Security, Medicare, and Medicaid statements, after you have reconciled them with your annual statements from these programs
- Any bills you receive in paper. Shred the previous year's stub when the same month pops back up on the calendar so you can compare your bills for future planning. (Comparing amounts also helps you detect usage to see if you have an inefficiency or leak.)

PAPERS YOU CAN SCAN AND THEN SHRED EVERY THREE YEARS

· At the time of this printing, IRS Publication 552, Recordkeeping for Individuals (which is available on the IRS website at http://www.irs.gov or by calling 1-800-TAX-FORM [1-800-829-3676]), states that you may shred support documentation for your tax returns three years after they have been filed. Support documents are any papers you used when claiming deductions or credits when filing your taxes—NOT the tax return.

PAPERS YOU CAN SCAN AND THEN SHRED AT THE APPROPRIATE TIME

· Loan paperwork, after you have fully paid off the loan and have received your paid-in-full statement from the loaning institution. Do NOT shred the paid-in-full statement.

· The deed to your home and records and contact information for any work and improvements made to the home and by whom. Scan the records, follow the instructions from your real estate agent for proper handling

of the deed, and offer all the other papers to the next homeowners of your property.

· All titles, records of repairs, servicing, and contact information of who did the work on your car(s). Scan these records, follow the instructions from your state about title transfer, and offer the repair and servicing records to the next owners of your car.

· Private school and/or college enrollment contracts and payment receipts for as long as your child/children or you attend the school.

· Membership documents for a professional or personal organization (like Kiwanis or Toastmasters) can be shredded after you have ended your membership in that organization. You also may wish to scan/save the notification you provided to the organization expressing your desire to end your membership.

· Service and rental contracts and agreements (like for phone service and apartments) can be shredded after your contract or agreement expires. You may wish to hold on to these documents for another six months if you do not receive a paid-in-full statement, plan to reinstate service from a provider within a few short months, or have not yet had your deposit returned.

· Warranties may be shredded when you no longer own the object. Some warranties can be transferred, so in these cases scan the warranty and offer the original up to the object's next owner.

· After the death of a pet, you can shred his or her medical, licensing, and adoption records.

· Annual federal and state (and in some cases county and/ or municipal) tax returns can be scanned and then shredded after ten years. No state requires you to keep tax returns more than ten years at the time of this book's printing, and the federal requirement is fewer than ten years. Check federal and state websites every few years to monitor whether this timeframe has changed.

PAPERS THAT CAN BE SCANNED AND THEN STORED INDEFINITELY

· Annual investment statements for retirement accounts, mutual funds, pension funds, and stock holdings

· Annual statements from Social Security, Medicare, and Medicaid

· Documents associated with your personal estate: wills, trusts, insurance policies, power of attorney, living wills, etc.

· Diplomas and final transcripts

· Paid-in-full statements for every loan and/or mortgage

· Medical records and contact information for your medical providers (such as what clinic has your mammogram images or MRI images of your knee)

· Federal and state-issued vital documents: birth certificate, marriage certificate, divorce certificate, military records, Social Security card, passport, immigration documents, etc. Again, you may wish to have duplicate copies of these documents and keep the originals in your fireproof safe. Since you can't get a "have on hand" duplicate copy of your Social

Security card and passport, it's best to store these items in your fireproof safe.

WHY SHRED?

Similar to how you want your information to be secure online, you also want it to be safe when it leaves your home to be trashed or recycled. The easiest way to do that is to shred any document with identifying information on it, such as your birthday, address, phone number, Social Security number, or any other obvious identifiers.

Digital Data and Security

Clutter is simple to spot when it's physical and taking up unnecessary space on your desk—printers that don't work and dead hard drives can get up and go. But when the clutter is digital and taking up space on your computer, tablet, or smartphone, it can be much more difficult to recognize or even consider deleting. Unless you need to hold on to very old data for your job or for legal reasons, it is okay to delete files you no longer need—clutter is clutter, no matter how small.

When working with these items, ask yourself: *Have I read the manual for my computer programs? Do I understand what my software and applications can do so I save time? Am I storing digital data (documents, music, images) in such a way that this information makes sense to me and anyone who may need access to these files?*

30 SECONDS

- ❏ Open the Downloads folder on your computer and delete any/all files you have saved elsewhere or have already processed and no longer need.

- ❏ Empty the trash folder on your desktop and in your e-mail application.

- ❏ Move a file off your desktop and put it in a more appropriate document folder (or delete it if you don't need it).

- ❏ Tag, add keywords to, and/or label folders for a few digital images in your photo software program so they are easier to search. Repeat this process in small steps until all of your images are labeled.

❑ Delete some blurry and unwanted images from your digital photo folders.

1 MINUTE

❑ Create an alias folder on your desktop for a subfolder to which you are saving documents while working on a current project. Or, if the project is finished, delete the alias folder from your desktop.

❑ Scan a document or two and save them to their appropriate folders. If suitable, shred the original documents.

❑ Open your computer's About This Computer (or similarly named) feature that will tell you what types of files take up the greatest space on your computer and how much free space you have remaining. Note this information and retain it for one of the projects in the 15-minute section.

❑ If you have a smartphone, plug it into your computer to back up and sync your phone's data or delete unwanted apps or blurry pictures.

❑ If you have a tablet device, plug it into your computer to back up and sync your tablet's data. If your tablet is your primary computer, back it up to an online backup service (such as iCloud for Mac products, OneDrive for Windows, and apps like My Backup Pro for Androids).

5 MINUTES

❑ Set a timer and work through your digital documents to see if there are any you can delete or move to a more appropriate folder. Sort the files by "last opened" to identify files you haven't opened in a long time.

❏ Sign up for Unroll.me to unsubscribe permanently from junk e-mails and "roll up" all the promotional e-mails you receive into one daily or weekly e-mail.

❏ Respond to as many e-mails as possible in five minutes. If any require action, set those actions on your calendar and/or to-do list.

❏ Back up your computer's hard drive(s) to an external hard drive and to an online backup service. Back up your computer to an external hard drive at least once a week and keep the backup in a safe place away from magnets. Then, set up an automatic backup or back it up manually at the end of each workday. Once you start the backup there isn't much else you need to do except for possibly closing out of the program.

❏ Identify files on your computer that contain sensitive data and add the file names and their locations to a to-do list to encrypt for more secure protection (see page 210).

15 MINUTES

❏ Process old e-mails from your inbox, then act on them, archive them, and/or delete them. Automatically archive any e-mails more than two months old.

❏ Train your e-mail program to automatically act on your behalf to save you time in your e-mail inbox. Read up on your e-mail program to learn how to take automated or customized actions (like applying filters) on e-mails that regularly come into your inbox. For example, if you regularly purchase things online and receive e-mail receipts for these purchases, you can apply settings on your e-mail system to automatically mark the e-mail as read, label/tag it as a receipt, and move it to your archives or a folder named "Receipts."

❑ Transfer all the largest types of files (usually digital photo files, music files, or movie files) to an external hard drive to free up space on your computer. Based on how often you move your computer from your home, a wireless network drive might be your best solution, or it could be a USB-attached storage device.

❑ Break free of checking your e-mail each and every time one arrives by setting a schedule for when you will check your e-mail. This might mean every fifteen minutes, or you might be able to check it only three times during the day. Your goal should be to check it when you have time to process all the e-mails you find, and only when it doesn't conflict with projects that require your full attention. Turn off notifications and instead set an alarm to indicate when to check your e-mail.

❑ Analyze your naming convention for documents. Choose one that makes it extremely easy to identify what is in the file. When drafting articles for Unclutterer and saving images to use on the site, I prefer to use the last two digits of the current year, the number of the month (starting with a 0 for single-digit months), the date, a dash, and a brief descriptive phrase. So an article to be published on January 1, 2017, about the benefits of uncluttering would be named: 170101-benefits. Naming documents and images in this manner will usually list them in order of date within the folder and also give you a reference as to their content, which will save you time.

AVOID TYPOS AND SAVE TIME!

If you are constantly typing the same reports, e-mails, phrases, or programming code, consider using a text expansion or text replacement program to speed up the process. If you have a Mac, the current way to add these expansions is to go into System Preferences > Keyboard > Text and click on the + sign to add your typing expansion/replacement. Then, in each program you wish to use text expansion/replacement, you may need to go to the program's Preferences and turn on/check the box for Text Replacement. If you would like a more expansive program, you may wish to buy and install a program like TextExpander, AutoText, or aText. At the very minimum, add common typos you make (for example, when I am in a hurry and mistype my name as Eirn, my computer automatically changes it to Erin) to keep you from having to delete and retype the word.

Secure Your Data

Securing your personal information is complex. Entire books and college degrees are dedicated to the subject. It's safe to say that in no way can I cover in a couple of pages all the ways you can digitally protect yourself, but I can provide tips to keep things more secure than the majority of people online (which will hopefully make you less attractive to hackers looking for an easy target).

PROTECT YOURSELF!

The most basic advice I can give is: Don't respond to sketchy e-mails, don't click on shady links, don't give out your extremely personal information, and run virus protection software regularly. These days, if you're running a current Windows operating system, you already have virus protection software on your machine in the form of Microsoft Security Essentials. However, regardless of your operating system, your computer needs a firewall.

My friend Alice, whom I mentioned previously in the Table of No Return section, is a top-tier digital security expert. She's so top-tier, she's asked me not to divulge anything more about her than her first name. I like to think of her as a legal hacker. So, when I wanted to know about computer security and which personal firewalls were good at their jobs, I asked her. She suggested ZoneAlarm and TinyWall as two trustworthy and relatively easy-to-use firewall programs.

She also had more suggestions for protecting your computer:

· Download and use a browser plugin that blocks ads and requires you to click on a Flash video before it begins playing. (Malware mostly comes onto computers through browsers these days.)

· Make sure programs you don't use are uninstalled from your computer, since the less program code your computer has to run, the more secure it will be.

· Check the privacy and security settings in all the programs you use and turn off features you don't use, such as "file and printer sharing" if you don't actually use/share files and printers in that program.

- Finally, turn off Bluetooth accessibility if you're not using it.

I also recommend using a password management program on all your digital devices that connect to the Internet. Programs like 1Password and LastPass require you to memorize a master password to access their services, but that's the only password you have to memorize. The rest are generated by the program (complex passwords with numbers, symbols, and letters randomly mixed together) and saved for future use. These programs are extremely easy to use, organized to save you time, and definitely worth the price.

After installing a password management program, log in to all the sites you visit and immediately change your passwords to as many random characters as your account allows. Aim for all your passwords to be of the best strength possible.

As you're logged in to all your digital accounts (e-mail, shopping, online storage, banking, etc.), be sure to set the communications from the service/company to their greatest level. If the service allows you to be notified each time you/someone tries to access your account, even successfully, choose that level.

In addition to creating very strong passwords for your accounts, Lifehacker.com also suggests picking the strangest authentication/verification questions you can. Stay away from questions like "Where were you born?" or "What was the name of your first-grade teacher?" and instead answer atypical ones about things like "What type of car did/does your grandmother drive?"

Finally, you should have and use an encryption program to protect the data in your most sensitive documents that reside on your computer's hard drive and online. My two favorite encryption programs, VeraCrypt and 7-Zip, are free and simple to use once you read the manual, so to speak. (The current deputy editor at Lifehacker.com, Alan Henry, also prefers these two, so I feel very comfortable recommending them to you.) When you're uploading scans of your vital documents to Dropbox or whatever online storage service you use, encrypt them so if anyone ever does hack into your account, he/she won't be able to decipher what is in the file he/she finds. If you already have sensitive data online, pull it down, encrypt it, and upload it again.

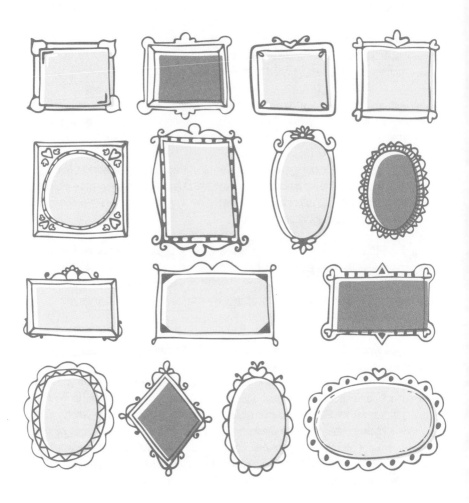

Memorabilia and Collections

When you hold on to memorabilia and have collections, you are curating your past through objects. These mementos from your life are important, but you can't let them negatively interfere with your present and future. To put it into perspective, not even the Smithsonian accepts every donation made to it—they want the really good stuff, the game changers, and the iconic emblems. They don't have space, time, and staff to preserve common and repetitive objects. When working through your memorabilia and collections, try your best to think like a museum (even consider having a pretend staff by bringing in an accountability partner to help you make choices) and keep only the items that you feel tell the highlights of your life story.

When working with these items, ask yourself: *Since I can't keep everything, is this item the best example of the memory I wish to be keeping? Am I okay sharing this item or collection of items with other people? Am I keeping these things because they continue to bring me joy and are documents of my happiness? If I'm not holding on to these items because of their significance in my life, why am I holding on to them at all?*

30 SECONDS

❏ Look at your memorabilia/collections. Is there anything in your collection that you can't remember why you've kept over the years? If so, get rid of those forgotten items first.

❏ Look at your memorabilia/collections and immediately get rid of any item that doesn't make you happy or add to your life in any meaningful way.

❏ Look at your memorabilia and see if anything could be repurposed to be useful. A large collection of old T-shirts can be sewn into a quilt. Your wedding gown/suit could be transformed into handkerchiefs or a baptismal gown or given away to someone who is in need of such an item.

❏ Take a picture of an object you treasure but don't want hanging out in your home, and then put the item in a box of items to give away. If the object is broken, beyond repair, or in terrible shape, I'm giving you permission to throw it away or recycle it.

❏ Look at your collections and name why you are curating these specific items. If you can't come up with a reason in thirty seconds beyond "habit," consider parting with your collection.

1 MINUTE

❏ When you choose to keep an object with your memorabilia and/or collections, remind yourself every time what your future commitments are to keep this object protected: proper storage, cleaning, transporting it if you move, sacrificing space in your home, etc. If you don't wish to take on these responsibilities or don't imagine yourself still owning the item in thirty years, reconsider keeping the object.

❏ Search archivist websites for advice on storing specific items in your collections so as not to accidentally devalue what you have already purchased/acquired. The advice may simply include a particular type of container, but it might also suggest specific housing to keep the objects safe, such as a climate- or light-controlled room.

❏ Scrapbooking can be a fun way to save memorabilia, but physical albums are often large, time-consuming, and expensive to create. If you like the idea of scrapbooking but don't wish to invest the space, time, and money in the hobby, consider digital scrapbooking.

❏ Call a trusted friend or family member and ask if he/she can be your accountability partner while you unclutter your memorabilia and/or collections. Having an accountability partner through this project allows you to have someone to tell your stories to as you work through your things. After scheduling time on your calendar for when you can meet, offer to return the favor if he/she wishes to follow in your uncluttering footsteps.

❏ Search online for the best way to clean items in the collections you display. Do you need a special cloth or oil, or can you use dishwashing detergent?

5 MINUTES

❏ Sort through a large handful of photographs and immediately shred any that are blurry or that you simply do not wish to keep.

❏ Study any collections you might have and look for duplicates and/or the items you like the least. Search eBay for similar items and see how much money they have sold for at auction. If the amount of money is appealing to you, consider selling the items you no longer wish to own. If the amount of money is quite small, list them on Freecycle or a similar service and find them a good home that isn't *your* home.

❏ Read a piece of correspondence you've been keeping over the years. Choose to shred/recycle it or save it. If you choose to save it, scan it and save it to your computer. Store the letter/card in archival-quality document protectors in either an archival box or archival-appropriate binder. Read, recycle or scan, and archive as much correspondence as you can in five minutes. Continue doing this project in five-minute intervals until you've worked your way through all your saved correspondence.

❏ Write/type guidelines for future acquisitions to your collections, similar to those a museum uses to determine what it will acquire and display. Just because you collect something doesn't mean you have to acquire every item you come across that would fit into your collection. Be deliberate about what you want for your collection and only add items that fit those guidelines.

❏ Tell your story about an item you have chosen to keep by writing it in a journal or in a document on your computer. If you aren't interested in telling the story of each object you have decided to retain, are you truly interested in taking the effort to properly maintain and care for the item in perpetuity?

15 MINUTES

❏ Based on your needs, acquire jars, glass boxes, or shadow boxes to hold your smaller trinkets and then fill the container with your items and display them. If an item is worth keeping, displaying it will give other people the same opportunity to enjoy it.

❏ Spend ten minutes writing in a journal or on your computer about why you have difficulty parting with sentimental objects. For the last five minutes, brainstorm ways that you can keep your attachment to the past but in such a way that your physical possessions won't clutter up your present or your future.

❏ Research digital scanning services (like ScanMyPhotos.com or a local photography store) and then follow their directions for how to prepare your photographs to be scanned by their company. Pack up as directed all your print photographs that you wish to keep, and then mail them or drop them off at your local scanning service. Then, over the next few months, spend a few minutes each day organizing, tagging, and writing keywords about each of the digital pictures in your digital photo management software. Afterward, you can give away the physical photographs to any of your friends and family who want them.

❏ When organizing the items in your collections or memorabilia, stick with the same rules you've been using elsewhere in your home: Keep like items together, organize items in such a way that the objects you retrieve the most often are in the easiest locations to reach, and label scrapbooks or other archival storage materials in such a way as to make it simple to get out and put away what you wish to access and easy for someone else to determine exactly what he/she will find in the book or box.

❏ If you are having a very difficult time letting go of sentimental clutter (not sentimental items that you cherish, but actual clutter that is getting in the way of the life you desire), consider hiring a professional organizer. Simply talking about your stuff with someone who works with objects for a living can often be all you need to get moving in a new direction. Of all types of clutter, sentimental clutter can be the hardest to let go. I certainly know it was for me when I started on my uncluttering and organizing journey. To find a professional organizer near you, search the directory on the National Association of Professional Organizer's website at http://napo.net.

BIDDING A FOND FAREWELL TO SENTIMENTAL CLUTTER

Saying good-bye to sentimental items is hard, there's no arguing with that. It's human nature that when you invest in creating or experiencing something, you feel connected to that item in a stronger way than if you hadn't. But the reality is that you can't keep everything, and if you're being honest with yourself, you don't want to keep absolutely everything you could possibly keep. You want to live your life, not curate it.

If you're having trouble letting go, start by reminding yourself that this is a normal desire. You're not a sentimental fool; you are human. Next, think about the life you want to lead and what sentimental items mesh with that vision you have for the future. Get rid of the things that don't fit into that vision. Finally, be creative with what you choose to keep. Have you chosen to hold on to all your handouts, assignments, and notes from every class you took in college? Instead of keeping a filing cabinet full of these papers, could you instead sort through them and choose only a few per class, and then put those papers in a single three-ring binder?

Or could you scan all the important papers and save them in a folder on your computer called "College Papers"? After you scan them, you can shred the original documents and simply look at the paperwork on your computer anytime you wish. Think outside the proverbial box and find the solution that works best for your sentimental items.

Is It a Collection or Clutter?

There is sometimes a fine line between clutter and a collection. If you have a collection, evaluate it to see if it meets the requirements for a collection. If it doesn't meet these conditions, either work to make it so that it does or get rid of the clutter.

- **COLLECTIONS ARE CURATED.** There is a purpose or intention involved with bringing objects together into a collection. Collections don't merely happen; rather, you seek out objects.

- **COLLECTIONS HAVE VALUE.** When brought together, the items in a collection have more value as a group than they do as individual objects. And this group of objects is worth a significant amount of money or holds a high personal/ sentimental value.

- **COLLECTIONS ARE TREATED WITH RESPECT.** Time, energy, and space are purposefully sacrificed to display a collection. Items in the collection are all well cared for and protected from damage and harm. Collections aren't haphazardly thrown in a box and stored in a damp basement. And a collection has a specific, limited, and designated space where it is displayed in one's home.

- **COLLECTIONS ARE SHARED WITH OTHERS.** There are a few rare exceptions to this rule, but the vast majority of collections contain a social element. Either the collection is displayed so visitors to one's home can see it and enjoy it or there might be groups of enthusiasts that can be found in online forums or at conferences who share a similar passion. Seashells from beaches visited on family vacations might be displayed in a crystal vase on a fireplace mantel or comic book collectors might attend a comic book convention together.

ADVANCED INSIGHT: It's possible for there to be clutter in a collection. If any of the pieces in your collection don't add value (monetary or sentimental) to the group or if individual pieces can't be cared for properly, those individual items can be uncluttered from the collection.

URGENT
HELP
★ ★

Safety and Emergency

First-aid kits, go bags, fire ladders, and other safety and emergency items in your home might not be used very often, but they are vitally important when they are needed. Making sure these items are ready for use and stocked with fresh and appropriate materials requires a little bit of uncluttering and organizing occasionally, but if/when the time comes, you'll appreciate your efforts.

When working with these items, ask yourself: *What are the most likely accidents that could happen in and to my home, and what reasonable steps can I take to prepare for them? Are my safety and emergency supplies stored in locations that are deemed safest by FEMA and other emergency response organizations? Are my safety and emergency supplies stored in an organized fashion so that others can help out in case of need?*

30 SECONDS

❏   Test the batteries in a smoke alarm and/or carbon monoxide alarm.

❏   Check locks on doors and windows. Make appointments to have any damaged lock or window replaced.

❏   Check levels on all fire extinguishers in your home. If any have indicators that are below the green level, schedule time on your calendar to recycle the canister and replace the extinguisher(s).

❏   Move any items that may be blocking heating/air vents and air intake vents.

❏ Move any flammable items that are in close proximity to your stove, oven, toaster, and other electrical devices that emit heat (including portable heaters).

1 MINUTE

❏ Check all the medicines in your home and gather up any that have expired. Then, take another minute to read the FDA's guidelines for proper disposal of prescription medications at www.fda.gov/ForConsumers/ConsumerUpdates/ucm101653.htm.

❏ Schedule a time to test your home security system with your security company. Do this system-wide test at least once a year.

❏ Test the emergency-stop mechanism on all automatic garage doors. Schedule a time to have the mechanism repaired if necessary.

❏ Flip up the edge of a throw rug, bath mat, or area rug and check to see if the underside of the rug has a grip texture. If you find a rug that doesn't have a grip texture on its bottom, take a few minutes later in the day to cut a piece of rubber no-slip rug pad to fit under the rug.

❏ Check the underside of your no-slip rubber mat in your bathtub to inspect for mildew and damage. Replace it if the mat is damaged.

5 MINUTES

❏ Research and purchase an emergency survival kit online if you don't already have one. As with other kits, it is often less expensive to purchase an assembled kit than it is to gather all the items yourself, in their appropriate amounts, for the number of people in your home.

❏ Look at the expiration dates on the food and medical items contained in your emergency survival kit(s) and replace any items that are past their prime.

❏ Wrap up slack in long cords with cable ties and feed the cables along your baseboards or at the backs of pieces of furniture to reduce chances of tripping, electrocution, and accidental stran-gulation of children and pets. See page 28 for more cable control suggestions.

❏ Organize your first-aid kit by putting like items together (gauze with gauze, adhesive bandages with adhesive bandages, etc.), throwing out any wrappers for used bandages, wiping out any dust or grime that has gathered at the bottom of the kit, and replacing any items that have been used.

❏ Schedule annual fireplace and chimney inspections.

15 MINUTES

❏ Take expired medicines to a prescription drop-off event or location. Check your local government website to learn where and when these events are held in your community.

❏ Store toxic chemicals and cleaning materials (rags, sponges) that come in contact with those chemicals away from food and in a place that is not accessible to children and pets. Be sure to label all containers so it is clear, even to guests, that what is inside is toxic.

❏ Install light- and motion-sensitive LED nightlights in all bathrooms and at the top and bottom of stairways (if possible). If your stairs aren't covered in carpet, also consider adding grip tape or a similar anti-slip product to each stair to prevent falls.

❏ Create emergency plans for yourself and anyone who lives in your home. Next, discuss the plan, who will do their best to grab certain materials, where everyone will meet up, all the ways to safely get out of your home in the event of a fire, where to go in case of a tornado, what to do in case of an earthquake, and other plans you feel you may need. Finally, practice each of these drills so everyone knows what is expected of him/her.

❏ If you or anyone in your care has an important medical condition, order yourself/him/her a medical ID bracelet or necklace that explains the condition. In the event the person is not able to verbally respond to an emergency medical professional, the medical ID should be able to speak on your/his/her behalf. There are many styles available and the amount of information that can be printed on the back of the medical ID varies by company/designer.

Create a Medications & First-Aid Kit

Every home has a place (or three) where prescriptions and over-the-counter medications, vitamins, bandages, and other first-aid items like thermometers are stored. Having items loose and on shelves in the bathroom instead of in a kit means that the person who needs the medicine and supplies has to come to where the items are stored instead of the items being brought to the sick/injured. Second, bathrooms are bad places to store medicines and first-aid items because warmth and humidity can damage these items, and warmth and humidity are synonymous with bathrooms. Having all your medications, vitamins, and first-aid items in a kit solves the first problem, and keeping the kit in a hallway closet near your bathroom is an excellent alternative to storing the items in your bathroom.

You don't need a metal briefcase to have a medications and first-aid kit in your home. In my house, we have two boxes with handles on their sides (so they're easy to carry): One is labeled "Boo Boo Box" and contains all the items someone might need if they are injured (bandages, ointments), and the second one is labeled "I Don't Feel Well" and contains all the treatments someone might need if they have an ache, pain, cough, runny nose, fever, or other minor ailment.

If you're an adult who has lived on his/her own for a number of years, you likely already own most everything you wish to store in your medications and first-aid kit. All you will need to do to create this kit is get a container or two, round up items you wish to store in your kit, and then make space for the kit in your location of choice.

If you're interested in beefing up the first-aid section of your kit to make it helpful in more situations than it might be currently, consider adding items recommended for your kit by the American National Standards Institute (ANSI). In the ANSI standards Z308.1-2009, section 6.1, they recommend:

- Absorbent compresses (something to apply pressure to a wound to help stop bleeding)
- Adhesive bandages (latex-free, in varying sizes)
- Adhesive tape (a roll or two)

- Antibiotic treatment (preferably Bacitracin because a lot of people are allergic to Neosporin and Polysporin)

- Antiseptic (antiseptic wipes or towelettes are really convenient)

- Burn treatment (spray treatment is very convenient)

- First-aid guide (picture guides are nice if you have kids)

- Medical exam gloves (latex-free)

- Sterile pads (different sizes are good)

- Triangular bandage (big enough to make an arm sling out of it; ANSI recommends 40 by 40 by 56 inches)

I also recommend a small bottle of hand sanitizer, cohesive wrap (it's like tape but sticks to itself instead of the patient), and a few instant cold and heat packs.

Step II

UNCLUTTER YOUR ROUTINES FOR A SIMPLER LIFE

Chris Guillebeau, author of *The Art of Non-Conformity* and *The Happiness of Pursuit,* on his organized routine when "moving in" to a hotel:

> I'm an active traveler. I spend at least 100 nights a year on the road, and often more—this year will be close to 150, I think. Most of my stays are one or two nights only, so it's not unusual for me to check into a different hotel every night for a week or longer. This routine demands a certain amount of order. I have to know where my stuff is!
>
> Upon entering a new hotel room (again, a common practice), I set things up in a couple of stations. My laptop and other work items go on the desk. My carry-on bag gets propped up against the wall, and I unpack whatever I need but no more. I try to avoid "spreading out" around the room unless I'm there for three nights or longer. This routine may sound boring, but it actually helps keep me focused instead of worrying where something is located.

Introduction

Routines don't have to be boring ruts full of doldrums and blahs. Routines don't have to kill spontaneity. In fact, routines can free up more of your time for having fun and following your desires.

The key to maintaining any preferred behavior is to make the action a part of a routine. If keeping an uncluttered, organized, and clean home is something you want to do, a few simple steps each day toward this goal will help that become a reality. The following section will teach you how to create routines that you will follow and that will help you free up mental space and time in your life.

Methods for Developing and Maintaining Effective and Efficient Routines

Routines are like automated actions in a machine. They're linked and repeated steps to help you achieve a desired outcome. And once you have an ingrained routine, you have more free time, less stress, and less mess in your life.

I like to think of routines as a little bit of work each day that allows me to enjoy enormous long-term rewards. They're simply the easiest and most productive way to stay on top of your chores and to maintain your uncluttered and organized way of life. Filing papers for only five minutes each day keeps you from wasting time searching for important documents when you need them. You also never have to waste an entire day filing, and you don't have to worry about a messy desk or an overflowing inbox. On days when there isn't any paperwork to file, you can have five minutes to do whatever you want instead.

An established routine of all the things you need to do before you go to work each morning can get you out the door faster and more smoothly. The same applies to routines you do each night before bed, which train your mind into realizing you're getting ready for sleep and help you to be more organized when you wake up the next day.

The goal of a routine is to make tasks become so familiar that you don't need to think about what you're doing while you're doing it. You can use the time to zone out or focus your thoughts on what matters to you.

ENGAGE AUTOPILOT

Making a change—any type of change—can be a roller coaster experience. One day you feel on top of the world, and the next day you feel like you're plummeting to the ground. Your energy levels go up and down, and so does your enthusiasm for instituting new routines. This is completely normal and an expected part of the changing process, whether you're trying to stop smoking or adjust how you complete chores around the house. The good news is that as long as you stay on the roller coaster, you'll eventually make the changes you desire and adopt effective and efficient routines.

Since the 1970s, rumor has been that it takes twenty-one days to adopt a new habit. For some people, this may be accurate. But it isn't the case for the majority of people. In 2008, researchers at the University College London found that **it takes most people a full twelve weeks (eighty-four days) to adopt long-lasting changes** in habits and routines.

Additional research has found that humans have a limited amount of self-control they can harness each day. You can do things to improve how much control you are able to wield—repeatedly getting a solid night's sleep, eating healthful meals, staying well hydrated, going outdoors for at least twenty minutes each day, participating in aerobic and anaerobic exercise at least three times a week, breaking up your workday into mindful and mindless activities, practicing self-control—but you will still hit a wall at some point. As a result, when you try to make a change in your life, you should only **tackle one change at a time.** Don't try to stop smoking *and* eat better *and* adopt a new morning routine. Choose one change for twelve weeks and master it, and then take on a second challenge for the next twelve weeks. You'll be much more likely to succeed at your goals when you approach them in this manner.

On the positive side, as you make changes and reach your goals, it becomes easier to make more changes. **Self-control begets self-control.**

Another important factor in adopting new habits and routines is to **know your desires.** Why do you want to change? What will you gain by changing? How will your life be improved? When you know where you want to go with your life, it's a lot easier to get there.

Also, it's important to **know how you work.** As previously mentioned, you need energy to complete routines. However, not everyone has the same amount of energy at the same time of day. Do the routines that you find most challenging and have the greatest desire to skip at a time of day when you have the most self-control and attention. Save routines you are least likely to procrastinate for when you're feeling mindless.

Another tip is to do your best to **keep your new routines and habits simple.** Start by incorporating basic routines and habits into your schedule. Master these steps and then add more to them as you see fit.

As you're coming up with your new routines and habits, and then later if you choose to add more steps to your routines, do what you can to **link obvious tasks together.** Professional organizer Janine Adams has a routine for taking care of her pets' waste. While walking her dog she picks up his poop in a small bag, then when she arrives home she walks straight to her cat's litter box and scoops anything her cat has done into the same bag. Next, she walks the bag back outside to the trash can, and finally she goes into the house and washes her hands. She uses only one bag, both pets get their messes cleaned, the cat's litter box doesn't get stinky, she only has to wash her hands once afterward, and the chore is completed in a minute. There isn't any additional thought involved about when she'll clean her cat's litter box because it's part of the same routine as walking her dog. Do similar tasks together, like cleaning the kitchen after every meal (you're in the kitchen already) and processing your mail when you walk in the door each evening (no need to bring junk mail into your home).

While establishing your routine and making it a habit, occasionally **evaluate it** to ensure it is working for you. Don't be afraid to adjust the routine as necessary to help you achieve your intended outcomes.

Finally, to help ensure your success with making changes and creating effective and efficient routines, **base your routines on functions** (such as "when I arrive home") instead of time-based tasks (like "at 7:00 P.M."). This is important because you may decide to sleep late or work late one day and your entire schedule won't be blown as long as it's based on functions.

To learn even more about routines and habits, check out *Better Than Before* by Gretchen Rubin and *The Power of Habit* by Charles Duhigg.

Sample Morning Routines

AT HOME (WITH CHILDREN)

- Wake up and exercise/walk dog (30 m)
- Shower and get ready for day (30 m)
- Cup of coffee in silence (15 m)
- Wake up children, feed pets, and make breakfast (15 m)
- Breakfast with family (30 m)
- Clean up kitchen: family joins together to unload dishwasher from last night, load new dishes into dishwasher, wipe down table and counter, sweep floor (15 m)
- Help children get dressed, ready for their day (15 m)
- Drive children to school and preschool (15 m)
- Drive to work (15 m)

AT WORK

- Arrive: hang up coat, turn on equipment, fill water bottle, and turn phone off Do Not Disturb (15 m)
- Work on most important task of the day (90 m)
- Process physical inbox: file papers, read print mail, etc. (15 m)
- Check e-mail and voice mail (10 m)
- Work on second most important task of the day (45 m)
- Meeting with department team (20 m)
- Lunch (30 m)

Sample Coming-Home Routine

EVERY WEEKDAY

- Remove shoes, put on house shoes (1 m)

- Hang up coat (1 m)

- Process mail: sort, open, write notes on envelopes, shred/recycle junk mail, and put mail into each person's in-home mailbox/inbox (3 m)

- Clean out purse/bag, process receipts, trash/recycle junk, and put important papers and receipts into each person's in-home mailbox/inbox (1 m)

- Charge electronics (30 s)

- Return lunch box to kitchen, empty out lunch trash, and put reusable containers in dishwasher (1 m)

- Look at weekly meal plan and determine when you need to start dinner (1 m)

- Put a load of laundry into washing machine (5 m)

Sample Before-Bed Routine

EVERY NIGHT, APPROXIMATELY ONE HOUR BEFORE BED

- General pick-up around the house—all family members participate (10 m)
- Fold and put away clothes from dryer (10 m)
- Run loaded dishwasher (2 m)
- Change out of day clothes and into bed clothes (3 m)
- Put dirty clothes in hamper/hang up "clerty" clothes (3 m)
- Pick out clothes for next day (3 m)
- Wash face, brush teeth (5 m)
- Secure doors and windows (3 m)
- Turn off lights (2 m)
- Read for 30 minutes or go straight to bed

Step III

SURPRISE SITUATIONS THAT
CALL FOR UNCLUTTERING

Leo Babauta, author of *The Power of Less* and ZenHabits
.net, on how he responds to clutter that delays or derails
his workflow:

> While I would love it if the world were without
> distractions, clutter and interruptions, I've realized that
> there is no such state of perfection. What works for
> me is learning to accept the world as it is, constantly
> reminding myself to breathe and accept. Then I deal
> with the clutter or distraction if I can, letting go of my
> desire to work without distraction, finding gratitude for
> the life in front of me.

Introduction

Becoming uncluttered and organized and having a home clean enough to share with guests isn't something that happens overnight. While you're working to get your home to your preferred state, life will continue around you—unexpected guests will appear, or you will forget to plan a meal and your family will be hungry. These things happen, but you need not worry, as the following pages contain suggestions for how to handle these situations and more.

Surprise! Guests Are on Their Way

Even in the best of circumstances when your home is tidy and ready for guests, unexpected visitors may throw you for a loop. Whether it's a friend dropping in to share a beer and catch up or your in-laws announcing they're coming for a four-night stay, you're likely to experience some level of anxiety about your surprise guests. Be not afraid! You have options.

PLAN #1: ANTICIPATED SHORT VISIT WITH 30-MINUTE NOTICE

- ❏ Sweep/vacuum the foyer.

- ❏ Put away errant items at your entrance (both outside and inside).

- ❏ Wash dirty dishes and/or load your dishwasher.

- ❏ Take out the kitchen trash.

- ❏ Sweep the kitchen and/or dining room floors.

- ❏ Wipe off the kitchen and/or dining room table.

- ❏ Wipe off the kitchen counters.

- ❏ Close all doors to other rooms.

❏ Check out the guest bathroom and make sure it has toilet paper, hand soap, and a hand towel.

❏ After your guest arrives, you can get out drinks and snacks and enjoy them in the kitchen or dining room.

PLAN #2: ANTICIPATED OVERNIGHT VISIT WITH A DAY'S NOTICE

❏ Sweep/vacuum the foyer.

❏ Put away errant items at your entrance (both outside and inside).

❏ Wash dirty dishes and/or load your dishwasher.

❏ Take out the kitchen trash.

❏ Sweep the kitchen and dining room floors.

❏ Wipe off the kitchen and/or dining room table.

❏ Wipe off the kitchen counters.

❏ Set up the bed in the guest room.

❏ Straighten the guest room and move anything you might need over the next forty-eight hours to someplace else in your home.

❏ Check out all bathrooms guests may use to ensure the rooms are stocked with toilet paper, hand soap, and towels.

❑ Straighten the living room.

❑ Straighten any other rooms you have time to address.

❑ Close doors to all rooms you weren't able to straighten.

❑ Once your guests go to bed for the night, you can attend to any other areas of your home you didn't get to previously.

PLAN #3: OUR HOUSE LOOKS LIKE IT WAS HIT BY A TORNADO, LENGTH OF STAY IRRELEVANT

❑ Meet guests at the door with your coat and car keys in hand, and guide them to a local coffee shop, restaurant, bar, or hotel. The reason they're visiting is because they want to see *you*. And they can enjoy your company at Starbucks the same as inside your kitchen.

❑ If your visitors want to stay a week, you can help them find a hotel for that first night while you prepare your place for visitors.

TV Is Calling My Name but I Have Stuff to Do

Unlike many simple-living advocates, I'm not opposed to the television. I view it as a form of entertainment, same as books and movies and going to concerts. A well-written and superbly acted program can be a worthwhile temporary diversion. My thought is that television is only clutter when you turn to it instead of taking care of your responsibilities or when watching it causes you to miss out on what matters more to you.

When television is tempting you with its siren call and you have responsibilities to fulfill, there are ways to handle the enticement. All you need is a plan.

PLAN #1: GO TO SLEEP

If you are really so tired as to not be able to do anything other than watch television, go straight to bed. I garnered this great tip from Gretchen Rubin about five years ago, and it has been my standard operating procedure since. If you can't be productive right now, you need sleep.

PLAN #2: USE TELEVISION VIEWING AS A REWARD

If you own a DVR, which I recommend you do, set it to record your program of choice. Then, turn off the television, complete the work, and afterward you can watch the whole of your program as a reward for taking care of your responsibilities.

PLAN #3: EXERCISE INSTEAD

Stand up and do some jumping jacks or run in place. Once you get your heart rate pumping, you'll feel an increase in energy and (hopefully) be motivated to get started on your work. Most people can only focus for about forty-five minutes on a single task before needing a break.

PLAN #4: LISTEN TO SOME MUSIC

Whatever music motivates you (for me, it's any song with more than 120 beats per minute and a super-catchy chorus), put it on and let it do its magic. My family has a playlist called "Cleaning Music" of our favorite songs that we broadcast throughout the house when we are taking care of chores.

PLAN #5: WATCH YOUR SHOW, BUT LET THE COMMERCIALS PLAY

I've never been successful at doing this, but for those with diligence and fortitude, you can have the best of both worlds. Watch your show and then get up and take care of your responsibilities during the commercial breaks. Vacuum the floor. Put a load of laundry into the washing machine. Race to see how much you can accomplish in three to five minutes.

The Family Is Hungry and I'm Out of Ideas

If you eat three meals a day, you have to plan almost 1,100 meals for yourself and possibly your family each year. It's a lot of planning, and it requires time, creativity, and mental energy to determine what you're going to do for all those meals. Even going out to get a pizza requires effort, and it's easy to see how people get burned out on ideas.

When you're ready to throw in the towel because you're out of ideas, start by making The Simple Meal. It's a protein, a vegetable, and a drink. That's it. You can prepare most proteins and vegetables with some spices and/or sauces to be fancy. (Well, fancier.) I suggest stocking individual portions of fish (like tilapia) and chicken breasts and some frozen vegetables in your freezer at all times. The Simple Meal is easy and doesn't take much effort.

Once The Simple Meal is on the table, eat it and brainstorm future meal ideas. If you're planning meals for family members in addition to yourself, go around the table and talk about your favorite foods (this is especially easy to do when you're eating The Simple Meal because you likely wish you were eating something more exciting). Pull out your favorite cookbooks or saved online recipes and look through those for inspiration. Try your best to come up with at least two weeks' worth of ideas. (Check out page 120 for in-depth meal-planning details.)

Until you get out of your creativity rut, repeat those fourteen days of meals. Take a picture with your smartphone of your shopping lists so you don't even have to re-create those after the first round of meals. If you're especially creative during your Simple Meal brainstorming session you could even come up with thirty days of meal ideas and probably rotate through them for five or six months before you feel like you're in a rut again.

Weekend Plans Fell Through

Weekend plans went belly up? Housework may not sound as exciting, but the rewards are long-lasting, and come Monday morning you'll feel like you have a weight lifted from your shoulders.

The following pages give a couple of plans for how you might structure your weekend at home. If one of these doesn't precisely fit with your needs, customize it or create a similar plan that works for you.

PLAN #1

	FRIDAY	SATURDAY	SUNDAY
MORNING		Get an early start and tackle work in your kitchen (pages 31–43).	Sleep in! Go to brunch! Do something worth an exclamation point!
AFTERNOON		Go out to eat, you just cleaned your kitchen, no need to mess it up right away; and then work in your garage (pages 163–169) or yard (pages 65–67).	Tackle the mess in your home office (pages 107–114).
NIGHT	Relax, catch up on television, do nothing.	Sort through a box of photographs or other memorabilia (pages 213–220).	Work in main entry to your home and get everything ready for the coming workweek (pages 13–18).

PLAN #2

	FRIDAY	SATURDAY	SUNDAY
MORNING		If you have kids, get them involved and work in their rooms (pages 98–104).	Address the mess in your clothes closet (pages 83–92).
AFTERNOON		Take a nap and then work in your bedroom (pages 75–80).	Go out to lunch and then drop off donations at local charities.
NIGHT	Take on the one area of your home that is driving you bonkers.	Work in your guest area to make it visitor ready (pages 171–177).	Get your bathrooms in shape and then enjoy a relaxing hot shower or bath (pages 45–53).

Glossary of Clutter-Related Terms

CHRONICALLY DISORGANIZED (ADJ.) According to the Institute for Challenging Disorganization, this phrase is used to describe someone with a long history of disorganization; a life that is undermined as a result of disorganization, combined with unsuccessful attempts to get organized in the past; and an expectation of disorganization in the future. It is not a medical diagnosis and it is most often used to describe someone who is perpetually messy.

CLUTTER (N.) A distraction. It is most commonly a physical possession that is unwanted, unneeded, and/or holding no value for its owner. It can also be an intrusive and unwanted thought, a negative relationship, a visual annoyance, and/or a commitment that is not in line with one's priorities.

DISORGANIZED (ADJ.) Chaotic, disheveled, disorderly, untidy, or slovenly. It is the opposite of organized. (The similar word **unorganized** means to not be a part of a labor union. The two words are not interchangeable.)

HOARDER (N.) One who has been diagnosed by a medical professional as having a hoarding disorder. A hoarding disorder is a pathological obsession with being unable to get rid of physical possessions. It is a complex psychological condition and treatment by a medical professional is strongly advised. This book is not intended as a primary resource for people suffering from a hoarding disorder.

MINIMALISM (N.) A style of extreme simplicity. People who live in this manner are called **minimalists**, and they eschew most physical objects, living with only the barest of essentials. Most unclutterers appreciate minimalism but choose to own more objects than just the minimum possible.

ORGANIZE (V.) To assign a systematized order to objects. Organizing is usually completed for the purpose of making it easier to retrieve items and then simply put them away.

SIMPLE LIVING (N.) The "Goldilocks and the Three Bears" view of an uncluttered life—not too much stuff, not too little stuff, but just the right amount of stuff to live comfortably and free of distractions.

UNCLUTTERER (N.) A person who chooses to get rid of the distractions that get in the way of what he or she wants to accomplish or experience in life.

Acknowledgments

Since I know you're leading a busy life, I want to first thank YOU for reading this book. There are billions of books in print that you could have read instead of this one, but you picked this up and invested your time and energy into it. I truly appreciate your choice and am grateful. Thank you!

If you aren't already an Unclutterer.com reader, I'd like to personally invite you to come and check out the site. The Unclutterer community is an amazing group of people—fantastic writers and programmers and extremely helpful readers who graciously add their wisdom to the comments. I'd like to thank all the regular Unclutterer.com readers and my writing team, specifically, who went above and beyond the call of duty for the nine months while I was writing this book. You all are amazing: Jeri Dansky, Jacki Hollywood Brown, and Dave Caolo.

A ridiculous number of people contributed to this book with their expertise, knowledge, and advice, and I am in their debt: Janine Adams, Emily Amick, Geralin Thomas, Mike Vogel (for introducing me to the term "clerty"), Gretchen Rubin, Chris Guillebeau, Jackie Kelley, Julie Bestry, Linda Samuels, Alice and Brad, Alan Henry, and Leo Babauta.

I'd also like to thank my brilliant editor, Cara Bedick, at HarperCollins, and my incredible agent, Courtney Miller-Callihan, with Sanford J. Greenburger Associates. Working with you both on this project was like wrapping myself in my favorite blanket. I'm so glad the band got back together to make this book happen. I adore and am in awe of you both!

Tremendous thanks to Deb Brody at William Morrow, who supported this project from the beginning, and to William Ruoto, Andrea Molitor, Laura Cherkas, Kate Schafer, and Paul Lamb.

Most important, to my friends and family who were patient and understanding with me through this process: You all deserve loyalty awards for how great you are. And specifically to Kara Heitz, Keith Whyte, Cherilyn Cepriano, Amanda Boatright, Kristin Betz, and Krystal Slivinski, for keeping me somewhat social and certainly entertained. Mom and Dad, you know how much I appreciate you, and if you have forgotten for even a second how much I admire you, just flip to the dedication at the front of this book. And to my brilliant and adorable husband, PJ, and our two incredible children, I wouldn't be living this amazing dream without you. I can't describe with words my love for you three.

This book was written on a 2012 MacBook Air and a good chunk of it was written to the music of the Bleachers, Hozier, and a playlist some kind soul posted on Spotify of all the songs mentioned in *Mo' Meta Blues: The World According to Questlove*. Coffee also played a major role in this text's completion.

Index

A

Adams, Janine, 183
aluminum foil, 40
Amick, Emily, 49
any room
  books and entertainment,
    185–90
  cleanup tasks, 69–71
  digital data and security, 205–11
  memorabilia and collections,
    213–20
  papers, bills, and subscriptions,
    193–203
apps, for home office, 114–15
artwork, bedroom, 79

B

Babauta, Leo, 241
baking soda, 37
bank statements, 194–95, 199
bathroom, 45–53
bedrooms
  guest, 171–77
  master, 75–80
  preteen and teen, 101–4
  small children, 95–98
before-bed routines, 239
Bestry, Julie, 14
bill-paying, 194–95, 199
books and entertainment, 28–29,
  185–90

buffets and sideboards, 26
bulk purchases, 151–52

C

cables, charging, 110
cables, media center, 28–29
canola oil, 39
carbon monoxide alarms, 223
cars, 163, 165, 166
car service records, 201
catalogs, 193, 196, 198
charging stations, 25
children
  bedrooms, 95–98
  cleaning skills for, 98–99
  morning routines with, 237
china and crystal, 58
closets, clothes, 83–92
clothes
  closet organization, 83–92
  laundry, 137–44
  owning fewer, 141
  wearing fewer, 142
club soda, 38
coffee tables, 25
collections and memorabilia,
  213–20
coming-home routines, 238
computers
  apps for, 114–15
  avoiding typos, 209

computers, *con't*
    data and file organization, 205–8
    digital security and, 210–11
cooking
    how to approach, 123–24
    meal planning, 120–22, 253–54
couches, 26
crystal and china, 58
curtains, sun-blocking, 80

D

decorative elements, 26
desk drawer organizers, 103
dictation apps, 114
digital data and security, 205–11
digital scanning services, 217
dining room, 55–63
dishwasher, 40
dishwashing soap, 39–40
documents, vital, 196, 202
Duhigg, Charles, 236

E

e-mails, 207–8
emergency and safety items, 223–28
encryption programs, 211
end tables, 25
entertainment and books, 28–29,
    185–90
entryway, 13–18
exercise, 250

F

family meals, 120–22, 253–54
fax apps, 115

fire extinguishers, 223
firewall programs, 210
first-aid kits, 223, 225, 227–28
food
    as cleaning agents, 37–39
    cooking strategies, 123–24
    meal planning, 120–22,
        253–54
    pantry organization, 117–19
    refrigerator makeover, 41–43
furniture, storage in, 25–26

G

garage, 163–69
gift-wrapping supplies, 130–31
guest bedroom, 171–77
guests, unexpected, 245–47
Guillebeau, Chris, 229

H

habits. *See* routines
hallways and stairs, 155–60
hampers, 142
hangers, 86
hardware and tools, 147–52
Henry, Alan, 211
hobby workspace, 127–31
home office, 107–14. *See also*
    computers
homeowner records, 200–201
home security systems, 224
hotels
    lotions and shampoos, 48
    move-in routine for, 229
    using ideas from, 79–80

K

Kelley, Jackie, 14
kitchen, 31–43
knife skills, 123–24

L

laundry room, 137–44
lemon juice, 38
lighting, bedroom, 79
living room, 21–29
loan paperwork, 200
lotions, from hotels, 48
lunch-making kits, 35

M

magazines, 195–96, 197, 198
makeup, replacing, 49–51
master bedroom, 75–80
meal planning, 120–22, 253–54
media center cables, 28–29
medical ID bracelets, 226
medications, 224, 225, 227–28
memorabilia and collections, 213–20
microwave, 40
money, finding, 14
morning routines, 237
music, 250

N

nightstands, 80
nighttime routines, 239
nursery, 95–97

O

oats, steel-cut, 38

olive oil, 39
one-minute rule, 73
ottomans, 25
outside spaces, 65–67

P

pantry
    decluttering tasks, 117–24
    meal planning, 120–22, 253–54
papers, bills, and subscriptions
    decluttering tasks, 193–97
    to recycle or shred, 198
    to scan, then shred, 198–202
    to scan, then store, 202–3
password management programs, 211
pet places, 179–81
photocopying apps, 115
photographs
    apps for, 114
    online, managing, 205–6, 208, 217
    scanning, 217
    throwing away, 215
pockets, emptying, 14
preteens, 99, 101–4
professional organizers, 217

R

rags, uses for, 33
refrigerator makeover, 41–43
routines
    before-bed, 239
    coming-home, 238
    developing and maintaining,
        233–36
    at home, with children, 237

routines, *con't*
    for hotel rooms, 229
    morning, 237
    at work, 237
Rubin, Gretchen, 73, 236

S
safety and emergency items, 223-28
Samuels, Linda, 135
scanning apps, 114
scanning services, 217
scrapbooking, 215
security, digital, 205-11
security systems, for home, 224
sentimental clutter, 218-20
shampoos, from hotels, 48
sheet sets, 78
shelving, 26
shirts, iron-free, 141
shredders, 10-11
signed document apps, 115
slacks, iron-free, 141
sleep, 249
smartphones, 114-15, 206
smoke alarms, 223
socks, 141
sponge systems, 36
stairs and hallways, 155-60
stash busting, 132-33
storage ideas
    bathroom, 53
    desk drawer organizer, 103
    double-duty furniture, 25-26
    garage, 168

nightstand, 80
refrigerators, 42-43
surprise situations
    resisting temptation to watch TV, 249-50
    running out of meal ideas, 253-54
    unexpected guests, 245-47
    weekend plans fell through, 257-59

T
tables, clearing clutter from, 159-60
tablet devices, 206
tax returns, 195, 200, 202
teenagers, 99, 101-4
television, 249-50
text expansion/replacement programs, 209
thermometers, 43
The Simple Meal, 253-54
to-do list apps, 114
to-do lists, creating, 110-11
tools and hardware, 147-52
toxic chemicals, 225
typos, 209

U
Unclutterer motto, 10
underwear, 141

V
vases, 27
vinegar, 37
virus protection software, 210
voice messages to text apps, 115

W

water, boiling, 37–38

weekend projects

bathroom supplies, 52–53

clothes closets, 90–92

cluttered entryway table,
159–60

digitizing bookshelf, 189–90

entryways, 18

garage, 167–69

guest bedroom, 175–77

hobby workspace, 132–33

home offices, 112–13

large amounts of laundry, 143–44

master bedroom, 79–80

media center cables, 28–29

medications and first-aid kit,
227–28

refrigerators, 41–43

securing personal information,
210–11

when weekend plans fall through,
257–59

white vinegar, 37

work routines, 237

wrapping supplies, 130–31

Y

yogurt, as cleaning agent, 38

Z

zip ties, 29

About the Author

ERIN ROONEY DOLAND is professionally known for being editor in chief of Unclutterer.com, a website providing daily articles on home and office organization. She is also the author of *Unclutter Your Life in One Week* (Gallery Books, 2009) and an essay contributor to *Manage Your Day-to-Day* (Amazon Publishing, 2013).

She received her undergraduate degree from the University of Kansas, William Allen White School of Journalism, and her master's degree from Johns Hopkins University. She is a writer, productivity consultant, and lecturer. She and her husband, son, and daughter reside in the Washington, D.C., metropolitan area.

In addition to her work at Unclutterer, Erin has appeared in publications including *Better Homes and Gardens, Family Circle, Real Simple, Woman's Day, Martha Stewart Living,* the *New York Times, Wired,* the *Washington Post, O: The Oprah Magazine, House Beautiful, USA Today, USA Weekend, Parade, Women's Health,* and many others. She has been a guest on *The Rachael Ray Show, WGN Midday News,* Martha Stewart Living Radio, and CBC Radio.